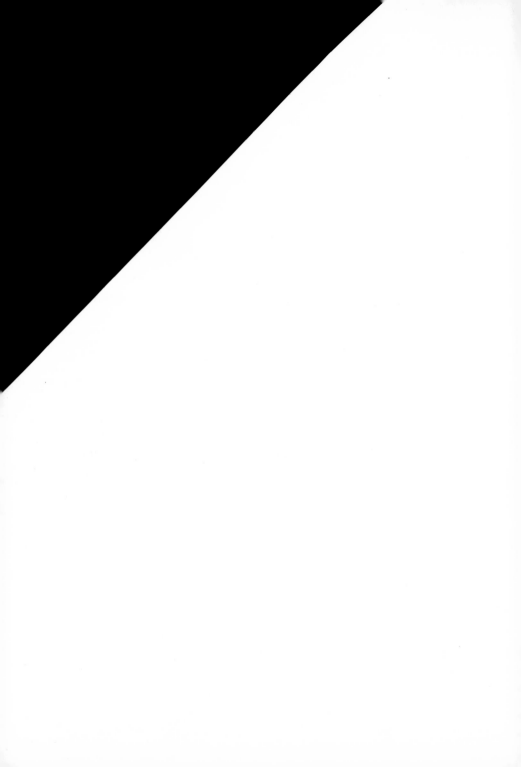

THE KING OF
SKID ROW

THE KING OF SKID ROW

John Bacich and the
Twilight Years of Old Minneapolis

JAMES ELI SHIFFER

University of Minnesota Press
Minneapolis
London

Frontispiece: Ted Evenson leans on the counter at Rex Liquors, John Bacich's liquor store at 201 Nicollet Avenue South. He lived at Johnny's hotel down the street and was a good carpenter when he wasn't drinking. Courtesy of John and Barbara Bacich.

Copyright 2016 by James Eli Shiffer

Published by the University of Minnesota Press
111 Third Avenue South, Suite 290
Minneapolis, MN 55401-2520
http://www.upress.umn.edu

Library of Congress Cataloging-in-Publication Data

Names: Shiffer, James Eli, author.
Title: The King of Skid Row : John Bacich and the twilight years of old Minneapolis / James Eli Shiffer.
Description: Minneapolis : University of Minnesota Press, 2016. | Includes bibliographical references and index.
Identifiers: LCCN 2015039581 | ISBN 978-0-8166-9829-5 (hc)
Subjects: LCSH: Bacich, John, 1919–2012. | Businessmen—Minnesota—Biography. | Skid row—Minnesota—Minneapolis—History. | Gateway District (Minneapolis, Minn.)—History. | Minneapolis (Minn.)—History.
Classification: LCC HV4506.M6 S55 2016 | DDC 362.5/928092—dc23
LC record available at http://lccn.loc.gov/2015039581

Printed in the United States of America on acid-free paper

The University of Minnesota is an equal-opportunity educator and employer.

22 21 20 19 18 17 16   10 9 8 7 6 5 4 3 2 1

CONTENTS

⇒ Prologue ⇐

A BUM'S PARADISE

On All Saints' Day 2014, in a corner of downtown Minneapolis normally deserted on a Saturday afternoon, a line of men and women formed on the sidewalk in front of the old *Star Tribune* headquarters at 425 Portland Avenue. They had come to pay their last respects to this building, where most of them had worked at one time or another, some for decades. They knew the place would be torn down within months to make way for a park. The demolition of the once-mighty *Star Tribune* headquarters was a sign of both the newspaper's diminished fortunes and the city's incessant drive to renew itself by making rubble of its past. Joining the line on the sidewalk that day, I remembered the first time I had come to work there nine years earlier, when I gazed up at the towering five-story limestone-and-black-granite facade. My eyes were drawn to the six stone medallions denoting the bounties of Minnesota (mining, logging, milling, agriculture, dairy, fish) and STAR AND TRIBUNE in raised stone letters protruding from its highest point. Occupying an entire city block, the building radiated power and permanence and consequence. After a career at small papers housed in buildings that looked like enlarged air conditioners, I could tilt my head back to look at that facade and think: this is a big-city newspaper.

In the cold sun of that November afternoon, I knew better. Workers had already jackhammered the six medallions off the facade and placed them in storage. They had tried to do the same with the stone letters, but they had fallen apart and were unceremoniously tossed in a dumpster. Whereas before it had presided over the city, the facade now awaited the wrecking ball that had already leveled all the buildings around it. Inside, the building lacked even that faded majesty. The presses that used to shake the entire block had been moved to a warehouse in north Minneapolis in 1987. The *Star Tribune* newsroom and business and circulation staffs now operated in mouse-infested offices with iffy plumbing and a basement full of abandoned furniture.

The occasion that day was billed as a "homecoming." It felt equal parts family reunion and funeral, albeit a funeral for someone who died at a ripe old age. Everyone who came received a laminated color photograph of the doomed building, a commemorative newspaper, and the opportunity to munch hors d'oeuvres, drink coffee, reminisce with old buddies, and mill around the cubicles and meeting rooms. At 2 p.m., a few hundred past and present employees took their seats in the fourth-floor cafeteria, where the newspaper's current leaders would give brief remarks. First, a stoop-shouldered man with white hair moved quickly to the podium, grabbed the microphone, and faced the audience. He got a brief introduction but did not need one, for he was the most famous journalist who had ever worked at 425 Portland Avenue.

Sid Hartman, sportswriter, onetime owner of the Minneapolis Lakers, TV and radio personality, was immortalized in a bronze statue that stood on the other side of downtown, next to the home of the NBA Timberwolves and down the street from the Minnesota Twins' ballpark. Here he was in the flesh, seventy years to the day that he first came to work at the paper, a few months from his ninety-fifth birthday and showing no signs of retirement. Sid didn't want to talk about any of that. He wanted to pay homage to the onetime titan of the *Star and Tribune*, John Cowles Sr., Minnesota's William Randolph Hearst and the patriarch of the newspaper's family owners until his death in 1983. Sid credited Cowles with bringing the Vikings and the Twins to Minnesota. Cowles did something else for his city, Sid said, his voice rising. "Washington Avenue was a bum's paradise," he said. That mattered because Washington Avenue was one of the city's central thoroughfares, smack in the middle of downtown Minneapolis. In

Sid's telling, that problem was so vexing to Cowles that he gave his second-in-command, Joyce Swan, a one-year leave of absence from the media empire to lobby Washington for the money to fix this part of town. Swan's pressure paid off, the politicians acted, and the bums were evicted forever. Then Sid spoke directly to the ghost of John Cowles Sr.: "Thank you for what you did."

Chances are, anyone in that room under sixty had no idea what he was talking about. In the 1950s, when Sid was still in his early career at the paper, Washington Avenue was Minneapolis's Skid Row—a Babylon of bars, liquor stores, flophouses, rescue missions, pawnshops, and diners packed together in the city's oldest commercial blocks. The neighborhood resisted gentrification efforts for years, until finally the money came through to do something radical. What was then the largest downtown urban renewal project in American history wiped out 40 percent of downtown Minneapolis. In only three years, demolition crews took down 186 buildings—every structure on the blocks where Washington, Nicollet, and Hennepin Avenues came together. It was replaced by a model for the 1960s downtown: parking ramps, high-rise apartments, blocky office towers, tidy green spaces, concrete plazas. It seemed fitting that Sid told his story in a now-obsolete building standing in the way of the city's next transformation. Through the windows behind him, I could see the prow of the half-built billion-dollar Vikings football stadium looming over Downtown East, and two Wells Fargo bank towers were visible rising just to the north. In less than a year, the Cowles castle would fall, the newspaper era at 425 Portland would end after ninety-six years, and the *Star Tribune* would move into rented space four blocks away.

After Sid's talk, I made my way through the crowd and asked him if he thought the destruction of the old Lower Loop had gone too far. He ignored the question and kept moving. I don't blame him. Most people who remember the littered alleys and panhandlers and pissing drunks said good riddance to that era. But as a newspaper building is to the journalism committed inside it, a bum's paradise is far more than the sum of its bricks and broken bottles. It has a hold on a city that will never let go. I learned this from the King of Skid Row himself.

Snapshots

A year or so after I moved to Minnesota to work at the *Star Tribune*, a friend lent me a grainy videocassette of a thirty-minute film titled *Skidrow*. It was assembled from home movies shot by a guy named John A. Bacich more than fifty years ago, in color but, curiously, with no sound other than the narration by a rough-hewn voiceover that seemed lifted from film noir. From the first moment I pressed the play button on my VCR, Johnny's movie carried me into a lost world that to this day I haven't quite been able to leave.

For a brief time in 1950s America, when people were fleeing cities down brand-new highways to brand-new suburbs, Johnny moved in the opposite direction and opened a liquor store, a bar, and a flophouse in the grittiest quarter of Minneapolis. The place changed him, like it did everyone who lived or worked there, but in his case, he ascended to a position of his own creation. John Bacich became Johnny Rex, the King of Skid Row. For some reason I still don't quite understand, Johnny felt the need to document his subjects. Whenever something was going on, which was almost always on Washington Avenue, Johnny grabbed his Bell & Howell movie camera and ran outside to roll film. The men of Skid Row jostled and guzzled, wrestled and hugged, lived and died in front of Johnny's movie camera. Inside his establishments, he made still portraits of each of his men, usually when they were seated in front of a row of liquor bottles in the back room. Then he got the film developed into three-by-five-inch snapshots with white borders. He pinned them in a neat line on the wall of his establishments, creating a frieze of weathered faces. When his businesses were evicted in the name of progress, Johnny took those pictures with him.

I had seen a few of those photos, published here and there, but wondered whether the entire collection had been preserved somewhere. So in the winter of 2009, I embarked on one of the many strange quests that I have devised to make my life more interesting. I was searching for a stack of portraits of men whose names I didn't know, whose deeds never amounted to much, and who died, as they lived, in obscurity. The pictures weren't particularly artful. Nor was Johnny known for his technique. His images made up a family album of people who had no families, men who had exiled themselves from what most people of the 1950s thought of as normal existence and taken refuge in the alleys and cage hotels of Skid Row in Minneapolis. I figured I had lost any chance of asking for help from Johnny himself, given how old he'd have to be by the time I learned of his existence, so I resolved to locate the missing photographs. I wasn't sure the photos still existed, or what I would do if I managed to find them.

That winter, I found a number for his wife in Florida and dialed. A telephone rang in a house on a Gulf Coast island. Then it stopped, and a recorded voice came on the line: "Hello, this is Barbara. Please leave a message and I'll call you back." I felt a little let down. Part of me wanted to believe that Johnny Rex was still around, since all my Google searches hadn't produced an obituary for him, and I was sure that his passing would have warranted a mention, somewhere. But I also knew that his relationship with his hometown newspaper might have been fractious enough that he would have boycotted us, even in death. I left a message, explaining my interest in the photos and my hope that Barbara knew where they might be, if they hadn't been thrown away.

She called back the next day. I introduced myself and inquired about whether she knew what happened to the photos after her husband's—

"Well, why don't you ask him?" she said. Then she moved the receiver away from her head. I could hear her speaking to someone else in the room. "John, there's someone here from the *Star Tribune* who wants to know about your photos."

A month or so later, a fat envelope with a California postmark arrived at my bungalow in Minneapolis. A documentary filmmaker had been holding on to the photos for an art project that never materialized, and Johnny made a call to San Francisco and told him to send the photos to Minnesota. After some negotiation, the filmmaker probably realized it was one of those things he would never get to, so he sent the pictures back to their city of origin. I ripped open the padded envelope and pulled out a black box, about the size of a thick paperback book, made of acid-free archival cardboard. I opened the box. Inside, curled against each other like old tarnished spoons in a drawer, were the brown studies of men, frozen in the 1950s. Their faces showed the wear of years of hard living. I saw gap-toothed smiles, deep lines, sunken cheekbones, inflamed noses, sometimes black eyes and fresh lacerations. They wore suspenders and plaid shirts, dungarees, occasionally a blazer, a collared shirt, even a tie. Most of these guys were clearly indulging the photographer, perhaps with the fear that if they didn't, that offer of a flophouse cubicle or fifth of muscatel wine would be rescinded. Some leaned back on a worn-out-looking couch. Others sat in an office chair, with a backdrop of shelves crowded with bottled liquor and wine. On the backs of the photos, sometimes Johnny had written a line or two in a neat script:

A hard worker! Married an Indian. From the South.
Wm. M. Johnston
Skeeter the Clown, tried to kill Johnson
Durrant! The tinsmith I taught a lesson to. He was artistically
   very talented
Headley the survivor! Both others were killed in car crash.
   Had an animal circus in Birmingham, Ala.
Very sharp. Died on operating table. A nice guy, Schneider
He lived in South Mpls and never returned tho only a few
   miles from his wife and home
Ted Evenson, A carpenter and a good one when sober!
A nice quiet sort of man.

Others have nothing written on the back. Were they so well known that Johnny didn't need to write anything to remember them? Or had he already forgotten their names? Many of the snapshots were taken in an office that had a plywood wall in which a rectangular section, maybe eighteen inches square, has been cut out. It's the kind of arrangement you find in certain diners, like the convenient slot through which the cook toiling in the back shoves the plates of greasy hash. In this case, Johnny had his men stick their heads through the hole to take their pictures. What you notice, if you look long enough, is what's pinned to the plywood above their heads. It's snapshots, photos Johnny took before that one. You're looking at a photo of the photos, like a hall of mirrors in which the reflections recede, smaller and smaller, but infinitely, into the distance. Then you notice that the photos in your hand are perforated at the corner by pinholes, or they have been pinned and unpinned so many times the corners have fallen away. You realize that this hall of reflections takes you fifty years into the past, back to a time when the largest city in Minnesota was home to the most notorious Skid Row in the Upper Midwest, the biggest main stem from Chicago clear to Spokane, and its king was a short fiery guy named Johnny Rex.

After our first phone call that winter day, I spent the next three years talking to this man, on the phone and face-to-face, recording our interviews, doing whatever I could to jog his recollection about a place that he had done so much to document but that had not existed for fifty years. He had reached an age when men do not feel self-conscious about pushing the buttons on their mental jukebox and replaying one greatest memory after another, as long as someone is sitting there to listen. I would never say I knew him well. Nor did I want to probe too deeply into the many sore points of his life. His combat experience in World War II was completely off-limits, his first marriage was clearly troubled, and he didn't want to talk about his children, either. Skid Row, on the other hand, had given him something like fame. Not at the time, but later, long after the Victor Hotel and Rex Liquors and the Sourdough Bar were closed and obliterated forever from the city's landscape, and Skid Row, also known as the Gateway District or the Lower Loop, was preserved only in

A gandy dancer poses for a portrait in the office in the back of Rex Liquors. Johnny photographed every one of his men and pinned their portraits on the wall. Courtesy of John and Barbara Bacich.

memories. Somehow Johnny knew people would want to know about this place, and that instinct would ultimately change the city's opinion of him.

Getting possession of Johnny's snapshots had a peculiar effect on me. I wanted to know everything I could about this place, and that meant seeing just about every picture ever taken of it. I learned that Johnny wasn't the only person who photographed the final days of Skid Row. Actually, the closer the end came, the more photographers swarmed into this doomed place, although for different reasons. In their decade-long crusade for the demolition of the Gateway, the newspapers went to extraordinary lengths to display the area's degradation. One photographer outfitted an alcoholic with a flashlight in his pocket and probably gave him some money to go get hammered. The resulting image showed the light trail of a drunk staggering down the sidewalk. Journalists became somewhat more professional as the end approached in the late 1950s, and the *Minneapolis Tribune* even commissioned a street-by-street architectural survey of what would soon be lost to the nation's first downtown urban renewal project.

In some forgotten boxes in the city archives, I found file folders full of black-and-white prints taken by Minneapolis Housing and Redevelopment Authority contract photographers. They had gone into every building in the neighborhood to document the decrepit conditions, and their cameras found every loathsome toilet, miserable hovel, ancient octopus-like boiler, rusty slop sink, attic splattered with pigeon excrement, and basement bottle dump. Many of the old storefronts and hotels were abandoned by that point, and for those that were not, any workers or tenants who happened to be in the pictures were entirely accidental subjects. It was as if the bartenders and seamstresses and potbellied pensioners were the last members of a tribe looking on helplessly as a colonizing empire flattened their forest. Even more photos are preserved in the pages of a dissertation from a University of Minnesota sociology student, Keith Lovald, who was deeply involved in a research project that aimed to understand why men lived in Skid Row. Lovald rented a room above a Gateway bar and used a telephoto lens to spy on the sidewalk. He caught a panhandler in the act. He witnessed a "bottle gang" in their alleyway ritual and captured the moment when a landscaper drove up and hired a laborer off the street. Other university photographers traveled to Skid Row as well, but they wanted to create art, not scholarship. Jerome Liebling arrived at the U from New York, where he had been schooled in the Photo League's socially conscious philosophy of photography. Liebling was well on his way to becoming a giant of twentieth-century photography and documentary filmmaking when he taught a class that encouraged his students and colleagues to shoot pictures in the Gateway, "a rough, densely packed, provocative arena, completely different from the established middle-class neighborhoods or the evolving suburban landscape of the Twin Cities," an art historian would later write. Their photos captured men in line at soup kitchens, dozing in mission dormitories, posing in doorways that would soon disappear. They stare at the photographer, or they look away, as their neighborhood falls to pieces.

One morning, maybe in 1960, one of Liebling's protégés, Robert Wilcox, stood across Washington Avenue and aimed his camera at a once elegant three-story commercial building. The shadows cast by the rising sun set fourteen windows deep in shadow, like eyes sunk in their sockets. A broken pediment provides an architectural flourish atop the cornice. Yet the building is sullied by a fire escape, artlessly bolted to the facade. It drops diagonally across the front of the building and ends at a platform above the first floor. Then you see the two garish storefronts—Senate Bar Liquors on the right and on the left:

Sourdough
Ketchikan, Alaska — Mpls., Minn.

A goblet overflowing with a great head of foam is painted on one side of the storefront. On the other side, an immense 10, the bargain price of that colossal beer. In front of the Sourdough are four men, standing in a tight circle as they wait for Johnny to open his bar, paying no attention to the photographer across the street.

Johnny Rex likely would never have known that his bar had been photographed had it not been for an exhibition of Wilcox's and Liebling's photographs titled *Faces and Facades* at the University of Minnesota in the early fall of 1961. A young woman supporting herself

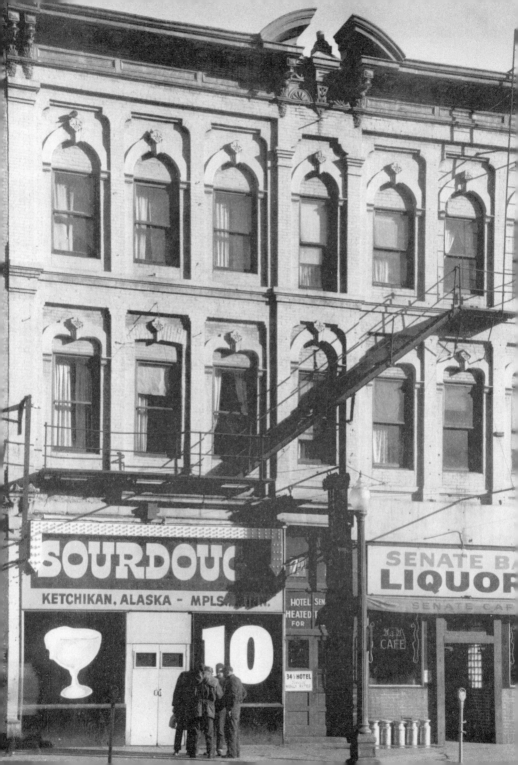

in law school by working as a waitress went to the exhibition and saw the picture. Then she told Johnny, whom she had met when she served cocktails at the Carousel Bar on Hennepin Avenue. Her name was Barbara Madsen, and she had fallen in love with this character, and before long, Johnny and Barbara would be married. For now, she wanted him to meet the art photographers at the university and tell them about all the home movies he had made of the men he called "gandy dancers" and the crazy things they did every day on Washington Avenue.

It had been a rough year for Johnny Rex, full of turmoil, personal loss, and trouble with the city. But if someone at the university was interested in his pictures, then he would oblige them. He met with Liebling. The photographer was so excited about Johnny's films that he involved his students and sent them to shoot additional footage, stitching the whole thing together into a coherent half-hour silent reel. The wrecking ball was already in full swing by this point, and within two years the buildings that made up 40 percent of downtown Minneapolis would disappear. The already rich photographic record of an American Skid Row would be crowned by this remarkable movie, although it would be a good thirty years before anyone else realized it.

The movie features several episodes of two men, Emil Teske and Nick Fiestal, both old railroad workers from Indiana. They are engaged in a peculiar kind of sidewalk wrestling that involves each one maintaining a tight grip on the other's nose. They do it in rain, snow, and shine, and sometimes tumble onto the pavement in their bizarre nose-pulling combat. They always come up smiling, though. This film is no syrupy view of the past. Violence and degradation were present

Home to two bars and a flophouse, the commercial building at 34–36 Washington Avenue South nevertheless radiates a faded elegance. This image was exhibited at the University of Minnesota in 1961 and brought together Johnny Rex and documentary photographer Jerome Liebling. Photograph by Robert Wilcox. Courtesy of Hennepin County Library Special Collections.

every day on Skid Row, and Johnny Rex felt compelled to film that as well, in blood-red Technicolor. Some parts of *Skidrow* are truly hard to watch. People had hit bottom, then broken through and plummeted into the proverbial basement. There's a dapper fellow in a cream-colored jacket and white fedora with a black band. John tells us the guy used to play piano with the Lawrence Welk orchestra, whose show started with rising bubbles and was beamed into TV sets every Saturday night across America. The musician shows off for Johnny's movie camera, flexing his fingers as if he's going up and down the keyboard in the air. He looks good now, John says, but he doesn't look like that after he's been drinking. Then he proves it, later in the movie, when the piano player now has a week's beard on him, his jacket is gone, and he's paying no attention to the camera. He's in a circle of men who are crowded into a dimly lit room. They're passing a jug around and everybody takes a deep swig. The piano man has a cigarette in his hand and an intense focus on the task at hand, and you can't help feeling that he's thrown away something valuable in this dark den of drunks.

Some people would have been scarred by these experiences. Joseph Mitchell writes about a habitué of Old McSorley's Ale House, one of New York's most famous bars. The man used to run a chain of Bowery flophouses, and he vowed on the day of his retirement to get drunk and stay drunk. "He says he drinks in order to forget the misery he saw in his flophouses; he undoubtedly saw a lot of it, because he often drinks twenty-five mugs a day, and McSorley's ale is by no means weak." Johnny more closely resembled another New York character from the same era, a saloonkeeper named Sammy, "mayor" of the Bowery and a friend to Weegee, the photographer behind the "Naked City." Sammy personally tossed troublesome drunks from his bar, but also was "a friend and ready to lend a helping hand . . . lending money so a man can get cleaned up, food and a room while he is getting over a hangover."

Johnny never succumbed to the bottle, or nostalgia. Yet he felt keenly that the city's forced removal of three thousand men broke up a real community and that someday people would want to see what it was like.

Nick Fiestal *(left)* and Emil Teske provided sidewalk
entertainment in Skid Row with a peculiar kind of wrestling:
grabbing each other's nose and holding tight. They lived in
Johnny's flophouse and were railroad workers from Indiana,
though their principal pastime seemed to be roughhousing and
drinking heavily. From the film *Skidrow*. Courtesy of John and
Barbara Bacich.

I was one of those people. I looked at all of these pictures and tried to reconstruct Skid Row in my mind—every bar, every pawnshop, lunch counter, barber college, job broker, secondhand store, storefront mission—and then searched my city for some vestige of it. All I could find were the same blank concrete walls and asphalt parking stalls that Minneapolis felt were such an improvement over its historic streetscape. "Not a trace of it now," Johnny told me in his movie, and he was right, but I kept looking and keep looking.

This book is my attempt to rebuild that place and understand what happened there in its final days with what I've learned from two dozen conversations with Johnny in the twilight of his life, along with old newspaper clippings, academic studies, city reports, other history books, and hundreds and hundreds of photographs. Skid Row was defined by its institutions, all of which Johnny Rex touched in some way. It offered men an escape to a warm sea of booze that would also drown them. It gave them a cheap place to sleep, provided they didn't mind chicken wire for a ceiling and the smell of men packed tight. It offered to save their souls and understand their psychology and cure their bad habits, or just give them as much alcohol as they could handle and then some. It was the arena for the worst and best instincts of human nature.

I probably will never solve the mystery of why Johnny photographed the men he called his gandies, but I know that act went to the heart of why he came to Skid Row and how he outlived the place, the men who lived in it, and his city's antipathy toward him and his kind. I am grateful Johnny Rex was willing to take me there, for one last trip into the end of an American Skid Row. What follows is the story of that journey.

This man played piano with Lawrence Welk's orchestra and cut a dapper figure when he showed up in the Gateway. "But after two or three weeks of drinking, boy, what a change," Johnny said, referring to the same man in the photograph below. From the film *Skidrow*. Courtesy of John and Barbara Bacich.

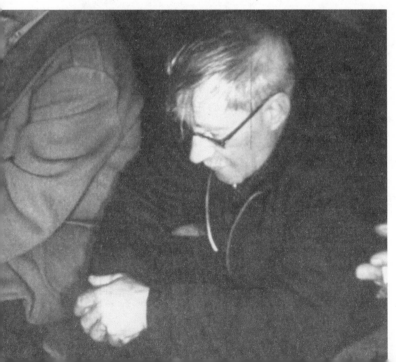

≡ 1 ≋

JOHNNY REX

"Down here on Skid Row, we're all thieves."
—Johnny Rex

In the warm seasons of his retirement, after his annual migration from Florida to Minneapolis, Johnny Rex commanded a table at the Starbucks Coffee on the corner of Diamond Lake Road and Lyndale Avenue. On that May morning in 2009, when I walked into the Starbucks at the appointed time to meet the old man in person, he sat at the head of that table, actually several tables pushed together to accommodate the collection of retirees, self-employed guys, hangers-on, and other folks that Johnny had accumulated like barnacles during his retirement years. He introduced me to the committee, and once I had shaken hands all around the table, Johnny got up and led me to another spot so we could talk more privately. It had an air of meeting with a mafia don, and Johnny looked the part. At ninety, he still sported a full head of white hair. His red collared shirt was unbuttoned to showcase the thick chain and silver cross around his neck.

The air was heavy with the bitter aroma of Starbucks coffee, as I prepared to present my case for letting me into his circle. Johnny Rex made it clear that he read my newspaper religiously, despite all the misery that hacks of the past had heaped upon him by their reckless and mean-spirited reporting. It wasn't until much later that I knew what he was talking about. The interrogation went the other

Johnny let me take his picture the first time I met him in person. He had just turned ninety, and we met at the Starbucks at Diamond Lake Road and Lyndale Avenue in south Minneapolis. It had all the atmosphere of meeting with a Mafia don.

way at first, him peppering me with questions about where I went to school, what I knew, where I lived, until he felt somewhat assured of my intentions. He somehow coaxed out of me that I was Jewish, and this meant something to him, for he had always respected the business acumen of Minneapolis Jews, some of whom ran businesses that were not exactly legitimate. I didn't have the heart to tell him that unlike everyone else in my family, I knew nothing about running a business. Johnny brought up the fact that he owned the building we were sitting in. The Starbucks just rented the walls and roof and store windows and the coffee-perfumed air. His presence from then on assumed a more imperial quality. He owned the place, and everybody knew it. I don't know if he got free coffee, because he was already drinking it when I got there. That's the only reason he didn't offer to buy mine.

John Bacich was a generous man, and he knew it, and it always twisted him in knots. He saw himself as a soft touch in a town full of layabouts with their hands out. Back in the Skid Row days, the mayor himself complained that his city had that squishy-hearted reputation; that it was populated by well-meaning folks who would open their wallets in response to any sob story. In the mayor's opinion, that was a big reason the center of Minneapolis was occupied by professional idlers, inveterate panhandlers, and human parasites. They were sustained by a river of charity flowing from do-gooder missions, spendthrift governments, and regular suckers walking down the street. Yet Johnny Rex arrived in the Gateway not to give money away but to scrape lots of money off those sidewalks and in the process banish his father's lingering doubts that Johnny could make something of himself. George Bacich's long career in immigrant capitalism had its share of ups and downs, but he nevertheless thought his youngest son lacked any business sense. Johnny was determined to prove his father wrong, and so he followed in his footsteps, even though what he had seen growing up should have made him stay the hell out of the liquor business. The retail liquor trade was corrupt and unpredictable. It exposed you to people's worst instincts and brought out their weaknesses and wrecked their families and livers and etched deep lines in their faces. And it could get you killed. Still, John Bacich kept getting pulled back into it, as if it was the Bacich family destiny, the only thing he could do.

That spring afternoon in Starbucks, I told Johnny I wanted to hear his story, from the beginning, so I could understand how he came to Skid Row with his dreams, his fists, and his camera. Lucky for me, he gave it up, all nine decades of it. As if he were waiting for me.

Way up in the northwestern tip of Wisconsin, back in the early part of the 1900s, there was a wild little town called Oliver. It was nothing but bars, saloons, and more bars, with prostitutes working the rooms upstairs, and they catered to lumberjacks, miners, and railroad workers, as well as the longshoremen from the nearby Twin Ports of Duluth and Superior. George Bacich, an immigrant from Karlobag, Croatia, was one of the leading bar owners in Oliver. He had to bribe five aldermen to get a liquor license for his Palimar Bar, and perhaps that inspired him to go into politics himself, because before long he was the mayor of Oliver. He had a paternalistic view of his role as saloonkeeper: you take care of the customers who pay your bills. It was a kind of compassion, but not everyone would see it that way. In the spring of 1919, his second wife, who had come to the United States from Poland, was pregnant and had no desire to deliver on a barroom floor. So when the day came, Victoria Bacich traveled over the St. Louis River to Duluth and gave birth in a real hospital to a boy they named John. She brought her baby back to Oliver but never wanted to raise her children there. Johnny's most vivid memory of the town was seeing a prostitute lying on a bed of broken glass outside a bar. Someone had knocked her through a second-story window. Johnny was maybe three years old.

His mother demanded that her husband get them out of that place and into a bigger city. Her timing was good. Prohibition had arrived, and rather than stopping the flow of alcohol, it opened the hydrant. Speakeasies and smuggling operations popped up overnight, and money poured into the pockets of those willing to flout the law. With the onset of Prohibition, George Bacich climbed the strange career ladder from legal bar owner in a corrupt and miserable little town to wealthy bootlegger in the corrupt and prosperous Twin Cities, the biggest metropolitan area between Chicago and Seattle. Liquor smuggled from Canada could travel undetected over the border into the wilds of northern Minnesota. The railroad junction of St. Paul provided a ready infrastructure for the illegal liquor trade, and the political culture was primed for corruption by a twenty-year-old policy of accommodation by Police Chief John J. O'Connor. O'Connor's policy toward the underworld was: Don't cause trouble in St. Paul, and I won't cause trouble for you. Naturally, organized crime flourished, and St. Paul became a sanctuary for fugitives and entrepreneurs alike. In about 1922, George Bacich moved his family—himself, his wife, two sons from a first marriage, and two from his second, including Johnny—into a veritable mansion in the mostly undeveloped Highland Park neighborhood of St. Paul. The house at 1925 Saunders Avenue had twenty-six rooms, at least four of them bathrooms, and four fireplaces, and it sat in the middle of acres and acres of hilly farmland that would soon sprout houses ringing the new Ford assembly plant on the Mississippi River bluff. For all the bourgeois trappings, though, the Baciches were still living on the edge. Not every gangster apparently got O'Connor's memo.

In the early morning hours, trucks would pull up to the mansion on Saunders. They had wooden sides, eight feet high, and inside were metal canisters of pure ethyl alcohol. The dangers of this business became terrifyingly clear one morning in Johnny's impressionable childhood. He didn't remember exactly how old he was at the time, perhaps five or six. The rest was impossible to forget. It was 5:00 a.m., and the sun was coming up over Highland Park. A big touring sedan that no one had seen before turned onto Saunders Avenue and parked in front of the Bacich house. Six men got out and moved quickly to the front door. They forced their way in, and suddenly the entire family was awake and hustled into the kitchen by the intruders. The boys felt the barrels of sawed-off shotguns jammed into their bellies. Where's the liquor? the men shouted. George Bacich told them there wasn't any. Johnny's mother somehow found her way to a telephone on the other side of the house and managed to call the police before the phone lines were ripped out of the walls. They snarled at her: What did you do? I called the riot squad, she answered. We better get the hell out of here, the robbers told each other. We can't find nothing. Before they left, they warned the family to stay inside the house. As they sprinted through the yard, one of them turned his weapon toward the mansion and fired one blast to make his point. Then they were gone. In Johnny's telling, his father got tipped off and made the liquor scarce that morning. How his wife, and his family, ever forgave him for not getting them out, too, he did not mention, but the terror of that moment lived with Johnny forever. He also learned something about his father: he was willing to take enormous risks to make money. That money came and went, in a hurry.

As the Depression hit, the family left the mansion and moved from apartment to apartment until they landed across the river in Minneapolis, in a modest bungalow at 3725 Twentieth Avenue South. The end of Prohibition in 1933 took the money out of bootlegging, so George Bacich turned his attention to real estate. People were talking about opening a canal that would give the Great Lakes a shipping outlet to the Atlantic Ocean. That could make the Twin Ports, the biggest docks on Lake Superior and the off-loading point for the forests, fields, and mines of the North American heartland, some of the most valuable land anywhere. George Bacich created a real estate company called the Seaway Corporation and started selling lots in Duluth and Superior. He branched out to South Dakota and beyond, and soon had offices in three states. His dad was a "big wheel," and Johnny was eager to jump on board. George Bacich still doubted his son could handle the responsibility.

He was willing to give his son a chance at wage labor in the family business. Even as he moved into real estate, George Bacich kept his hand in the liquor trade. In 1935 he bought the Gitchinadji Country Club, "The Gay Hot Spot of the North." It was a white-tablecloth joint built on the banks of the St. Louis River in Superior, Wisconsin, only a few miles from wild Oliver but leagues away in character. The Gitchinadji served a much more sedate clientele. Patrons toasted each other with thirty-cent gin rickeys or glasses of sparkling Mumm champagne to the strains of the house orchestra. At the Gitchinadji, Johnny learned the basics of the bar business, working side by side with his brother, George Jr. He waited on local vacationers and actual

TELEPHONE
4501

PRIVATE PARTIES
AND BANQUETS

WINE, DINE AND DANCE
AT THE

Gitchinadji Cabaret
SUPERIOR, WISCONSIN

The Gay Hot Spot of the North

★ ★ ★ ★

GITCHINADJI COUNTRY CLUB

OPEN FROM 9 P. M.
UNTIL 3 A. M.

OVER

GEORGE BACICH, JR.

MANAGER

DINING PORCH

Starting in the 1930s, George Bacich owned and operated the Gitchinadji Country Club, a well-heeled restaurant in Superior, Wisconsin, on the St. Louis River. His son learned the basics of the hospitality business there, although his father would never give him much authority. Courtesy of John and Barbara Bacich.

princes and princesses, serving them seventy-five-cent steak dinners with cuts of meat flown in from Chicago. This was about as high as his father would let him get, and Johnny's frustration was building. His opportunity to take command was coming, though, just as the world began to darken under the storm of war.

John drew a low number in the draft lottery in early 1941, and not putting off the inevitable he enlisted at Fort Snelling a month later, on February 17, 1941. At first army life was easy, and he was sixty days away from finishing his service when Japanese warplanes bombed Pearl Harbor. It would be another five years before he would leave active service. He was still stateside in May 1943 when the terrible news came that his brother George Jr., serving in the Army Air Corps, had been killed in combat over Europe. John shipped off to war in late 1944. He was a staff sergeant in the Thirty-Sixth Cavalry Recon Squad and the Ninetieth Infantry Division, commanding a tank that rolled through the bloody fields and blasted villages of France and Germany. Johnny told me his unit liberated a Nazi concentration camp outside Prague, but that was about all he would say. His wife told me later that his tank's job was to do reconnaissance until the Germans started shooting, and then to turn around and get out of there. I later found a photocopied paper in Johnny's files that gave another clue to the nature of his service, a certificate of merit from his colonel for "exceptional courage, initiative and devotion to duty" by capturing prisoners of war, evacuating the wounded, and establishing communications during a battle in January 1945. The only time Johnny let something slip was recalling how some desk officer in a bow tie, back home in the States, asked him what he would do for a job after his five years in the army. "What are you fit for?" the bureaucrat said. Johnny snarled: "I'm good at killing and murdering. That's what I'm fit for."

Other experiences translated more easily to civilian life. Johnny was a natural leader in the military, and men trusted him with their lives. He also had a wondrous talent for procurement. He was frequently called upon by commanding officers and grunts alike to acquire booze for official and unofficial functions. He always seemed to know how to find it, whether he was in a military base in Kansas or an

NCO club in occupied France. He mustered out as a lieutenant with a sterling war record that he naively believed would open doors for him.

John had no use for formal education. He hated school, as he said, with a "purple passion," and while he managed to earn his diploma from Cretin High School in St. Paul, his higher education ended after a few months at the Minnesota College of Business, where he found himself staring out the window at the girls instead of listening to the lectures. He knew he would learn much more about business out on the streets than in a classroom. John was willing to work hard and hustle. As a teenager, he and his neighborhood friends would jump into Lake Hiawatha and dive twenty feet to the bottom to retrieve lost golf balls, clean them up, dry them off, and sell them back to the golfers at the Hiawatha golf course. One time when he and a friend were diving for golf balls, a thunderstorm blew in. Rain started pouring and lightning cracked the sky and his friend ran for cover under a tree. Johnny stayed in the water. Then a bolt lit up the air, split in two, and smacked both of them on the head like a mallet. Johnny and his friend escaped with gouges in their scalps. It wouldn't be the last time he would be scarred on the job.

Back home in Minneapolis after the war, John finally felt ready to run his own establishment. His father set aside his skepticism and helped him buy the Savoy Restaurant, a twenty-four-hour hash house at Sixteenth Street and Nicollet Avenue just south of downtown. It was a rude awakening for a new businessman. Every one of his employees stole from him. Waitresses would serve steaks, collect the cash, ring them up as if they were hamburgers, and then pocket the difference. One of his dishwashers would smuggle ribs out of the icebox, wrap them in wax paper, and hide them in mounds of discarded potato peelings. Once the trash went out to the alley, the man would come back in the middle of the night and retrieve the purloined meat. John knew something was up, so he hid in the alley and at the moment the dishwasher showed up for his ribs, he came out of the shadows, delivered a powerful kick to his employee's rump, and told the guy to get lost, forever. After three months, Johnny couldn't handle it anymore. Maybe his father was right after all. Only ninety days in the restaurant business, and he was through. He sold the Savoy and set out with his young wife for California, where he thought he could make a fortune selling real estate. Instead, he sold insurance for a couple of years. His wife got homesick, and though it was sunny and beautiful in California, and cold and miserable in Minnesota, John agreed to give his hometown another try.

Not many men head to Skid Row to make it big. This was where lives petered out. For decades, the Gateway District had served as the hub for men seeking seasonal labor in the railroads, farms, and pine forests of the Upper Midwest. By the 1950s, those jobs were disappearing, and the Gateway District had assumed an air of inertia and slow decay. People from other parts of town only visited the place after dark to finish off their weekend binges with cheap nightcaps, or to take in a floor show at the Persian Palms. Aside from the shopkeepers and warehouse owners who could not afford to operate anywhere else, and the merchants who took the old men's pension money in return for booze, upstanding Minneapolis residents viewed people who wore secondhand suits and lived in stinking flophouses as distasteful and parasitic.

In 1952 right-wing journalists Jack Lait and Lee Mortimer published a kind of travel guide for sleaze called *U.S.A. Confidential*, and their chapter on Minnesota set their poison pens loose on the Gateway. Aside from prostitutes swarming Hennepin Avenue, they wrote, "There is a huge population of transients—railroad workers, migratory farm hands and roughneck woodsmen from the north woods and Canada, as well as drifting hoboes. Sooner or later, they gravitate to Minneapolis." There they would find a "terrible" Skid Row. "We have seen all the dives in the land, and few are quite as bad as the Chez Paree, the Bowery, the 114, the Persian Palms and the Arabian Nights, all of which cater to the lowest winos and the blowziest hags. A sign over the hotel bar proclaims, 'Rooms 50 cents. No questions asked, either.'" Lait and Mortimer blamed the situation on a liberal welfare policy and rampant corruption. "When the [pension] checks arrive on the first and fifteenth, every Skid Row joint is packed with elderly drunks, who end up in the sewers, broke and sick." Lait and Mortimer prided themselves on identifying suspected gangsters and other lowlifes by name, and their journalistic rampages left a trail of defamation suits. Still, their portrait of the Lower Loop had the ring of truth for many in Minneapolis who were intent on cleaning up the city's reputation.

As early as the 1890s, Minneapolis had recognized that its oldest quarter was becoming a little seedy. The city thought major public works projects would help. Starting in 1908, they enlarged the old Bridge Square, called it Gateway Park, and put up a Beaux-Arts-style pavilion seven years later. In 1924 private businesses paid for the construction of the $3.5 million Nicollet Hotel, which rose like

The corner of Nicollet and Washington was the heart of Minneapolis's Skid Row, also known as the Gateway District. In the mid-1950s, Johnny thought he could make it big there by supplying what the gandy dancers wanted and needed. This view shows Nicollet Avenue in the foreground and looks east on Washington Avenue. Courtesy of the City of Minneapolis.

After dark, the bright lights of the Gateway beckoned to both local tipplers and outsiders, who came here to finish off their nights on the town with cheap drinks. In 1953 the 24 Bar and the Bowery were at 24 and 26 Washington Avenue South, a few doors down from the Sourdough. Copyright Star Tribune Media Company LLC. Reprinted with permission.

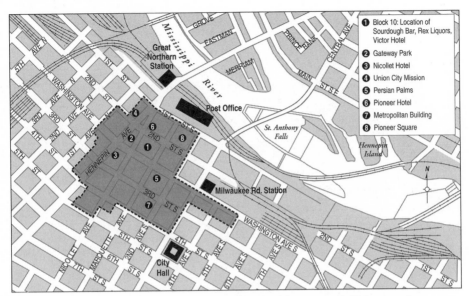

The Gateway District occupied the oldest quarter of Minneapolis. In the late 1950s, the city determined that virtually every building within the redevelopment zone would have to come down. Map by Philip Schwartzberg, Meridian Mapping, Minneapolis.

a fortress on the park's south edge. In 1931, on what used to be the most notorious street of brothels in Minneapolis, they built an enormous art deco post office, two city blocks long, and put a new park across First Street called Pioneer Square. All of these things failed to change the character of the place. City leaders wrung their hands, but the area now known as the Gateway seemed to defeat their every effort. By the mid-1950s, many forces were converging toward a solution bolder than anything the city had tried before. In fact, it was bolder than anything any American city had tried.

Everyone recognized that the survival of American downtowns was suddenly in doubt, and in some ways, these areas fell victim to American prosperity. The U.S. economy's boom in the 1950s was exemplified by the shiny streamlined cars rolling by the millions off

JOHNNY REX

27

Detroit's assembly lines, yet the growing middle classes were fleeing the once mighty cities. They could rightly point the finger at those Fords and Chevrolets and Ramblers as the reasons for the decline of downtowns, as the American love of the open road and ample parking found no satisfaction in districts built for people getting around on foot and by streetcar. The rise of the automobile dealt a one-two punch to cities, both by drawing away residents and jobs and by encouraging demolition of large areas to make way for parking lots and widened roads. In 1961 journalist and urban activist Jane Jacobs recognized that highways and other concessions to automobiles were "powerful and insistent instruments of city destruction." Eager to keep their central business districts vibrant, downtown boosters decided that nearby residential neighborhoods would have to go. They worried that female shoppers would be scared off by the prospect of parking in slum areas. Municipal leaders were desperate to keep their cities relevant. To do so, they decided their old quarters would first have to be destroyed.

These were not new worries, but this time, huge sums of public money were suddenly there for the taking. The largest public works project in human history, the Interstate Highway network, was reshaping America to enable suburban sprawl beyond anyone's comprehension. Cities eagerly tapped into that money to ensure the freeways were built through them, even if it meant bulldozing entire neighborhoods, particularly minority districts that lacked the political power to stop them. Federal laws passed in the late 1940s and early 1950s prioritized urban redevelopment, and Minneapolis eagerly sought that new money to replace aging workers' housing, much of it built in the nineteenth century, with apartment blocks of reassuring, modern sameness. In the planning dogma of the 1950s, the new was ideal, rational, and modern, while old buildings were "obsolete" and "blighted." A law passed in 1954 enabled federal funding for renewal projects that were primarily nonresidential. Minneapolis leapt at the opportunity to deal with its persistent problem. The city's central business district—its major stores, banks, hotels, and theaters—had long before moved away from the river and south along Nicollet and Hennepin Avenues. Still, going to the post office or either train station meant walking through Skid Row, and probably a gauntlet of rowdy beggars. In 1958 *Fortune* magazine could have been talking about Minneapolis when it declared that slums "are eating away at the heart of the cities, especially their downtown areas."

The crisis for Minnesota's largest city and economic capital had reached a tipping point three years earlier. General Mills was one of Minneapolis's bedrock businesses and a direct link to the city's milling origins. In 1955 the company announced that it would move to the suburb of Golden Valley, joining the massive flight of residents that was already shrinking the city's population from its 1950 peak. Minneapolis's leaders could look only a block away from General Mills' evacuated headquarters to see the saloons, the pawnshops, the fifty-cent-a-night hotels. No matter what happened, those institutions seemed stubbornly determined to stay put. Unemployed men idling on the sidewalks in front of crumbling buildings were constant reminders of a past that Minneapolis believed was holding it back from greatness. Robert Jorvig, the head of the city's Housing and Redevelopment Authority at the time, told me that Minneapolis was determined to avoid what were seen in the past as half measures. Skid Row just seemed to swallow up Gateway Park and Pioneer Square, and the gandy dancers literally pissed on the wall of the Nicollet Hotel. "You couldn't solve the problem unless you dealt with everything. I don't think we could have done anything about the Skid Row to preserve any part of that, and still get the new development." So, armed with federal money and a determination to start with a clean slate, city planners plotted the end of Skid Row.

It must have seemed crazy, or desperate, to imagine a business empire could be built in a part of town so alienated from the rest of the city, and with a "condemned" sign to boot. At this point, though, John Bacich had no pedigree, no wealthy benefactors, no connection to the Daytons or the Pillsburys or the other leading families of Minneapolis industry. He would surrender himself to the seaminess and learn to navigate the corrupt rules of selling booze in Minneapolis. He learned to stay on the good side of the gangsters who controlled much of the city's liquor business. He paid off the cops and gave money to the aldermen. He befriended the president of the city council, a former Golden Gloves boxer named Frank Wolinski, knowing he was the go-to guy for anyone who wanted a liquor permit. He got a lawyer who kept him out of trouble with the health department and the judges. The lawyer, Lewis "Scoop" Lohmann, gave his client a new name befitting his stature, because John realized he could be a king here, and he would love his subjects, and take care of them, in the way his father took care of the drunken lumberjacks of Oliver. From time to time, he wondered whether he was enabling their misery. But the men would always deny it and say just how happy they were that Johnny Rex was around to help them lead lives free of responsibility.

It was a measure of how much he had immersed himself in the Gateway that Johnny had no intention of helping the authorities clean the place up. Sure, he would let them go through his photo album if they had found a Mississippi River floater or were looking for a murderer. That's about as far as it was going to go. "Like I told this FBI guy when he wanted me to be one of his stooges, I says, 'Down here on Skid Row, we're all thieves, including the enforcers and everybody,' and I says, 'so don't you come around asking me to be a stooge for you!'"

Johnny's devotion to his gandies, captured in his home movies and snapshots, might have seemed self-serving at the time, but it would eventually bring him a lasting legitimacy that he was always seeking, in one of those strange turns of history that you can't make up. For those few wild years, he ruled the sidewalks, and everyone riding the rails into Minneapolis or ringing the big bell in the Sourdough knew the name of Johnny Rex.

These rough characters were hanging around outside the Stockholm Bar and Café, 33 Washington Avenue South, in 1953. The city worried that the streets of Skid Row were intimidating to downtown visitors. One journalist asked that year: "Who are these strangers in our Gateway?" Copyright Star Tribune Media Company LLC. Reprinted with permission.

≈ 2 ≈

THE GANDIES

The skid rower does not bathe, eat regularly, dress
respectably, marry or raise children, attend school,
vote, own property, or regularly live in the same place.
He does little work of any kind. He does not even steal.
The skid rower does nothing, he just is.
—Samuel Wallace, *Skid Row as a Way of Life*

The reunion took place on a summer day in 2009, a few months
after the meeting at Starbucks. I carefully placed the box of
curled, brittle photos in a messenger bag and rode my bike through
the streets of Minneapolis, around the old water tower on the hill,
across the bridge over Minnehaha Creek, and onto Harriet Avenue
South. I chained my bike to a sign pole, walked up to Johnny's house,
and knocked on the door, feeling as if something important was
going to happen.

Moments later, I was sitting down on the couch in his TV room.
The old man took a seat in an easy chair, and across a little table
crowded with pillboxes, the TV remote, and other detritus, his wife,
Barbara, sat down in hers. I opened the box and he picked up the first
one, straightened it out, and looked at it. This was the moment I had
been hoping for.

I could almost feel his brain spinning to remember each one. Some
of them were easy, mostly because he had taken the time to write

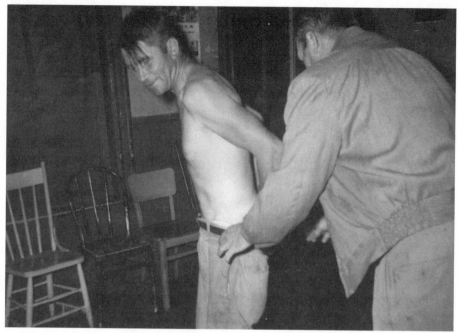

A gandy dancer named Jackmeyer horsed around in the Victor Hotel, 21½ Second Street South. He was best known for escaping from the drunk tank through a second-story window, landing on his head. Courtesy of John and Barbara Bacich.

something on the back. There was Skeeter, who once tried to settle a grudge with a .25-caliber revolver, but he only had a .22 bullet, which, fortunately for everyone involved, refused to perform. There was Art Durrant, the master tinsmith, who could fashion anything out of metal but gave up on his two jobs and his wife in Chicago to pursue a life of railroad work and heavy drinking. Then there was Emil Teske, one of the nose pullers from Johnny's film, who liked to walk to the liquor store in his underwear, no matter how cold it was, or sometimes a burlap sack with holes cut for his arms and head. He had a photo of shirtless Jackmeyer, best known for escaping a small-town jail from a second-story window. He landed on his head

Emil Teske tucks in his shirt at the Victor Hotel. The pinups on the wall were the only females the proprietor would allow. A sign warns residents: *All noises and TV must stop at 10:30 p.m. No exceptions!* Courtesy of John and Barbara Bacich.

but lived to tell the tale. A thick-lipped man in a fuzzy close-up was identified as Abel, known for his claustrophobia, which one sadistic gandy dancer surely knew when he once locked him in a closet. There was a man with fresh abrasions on his stubbly face. He was leaning back in a chair, with his left leg propped on a cushion. That was Jim Headley, "the survivor," so named because he was the only one left alive after a terrible car crash that killed Polack Mary and George Johnson. Headley hailed from Birmingham, Alabama, where he used to run a little circus that he set up by the side of the road. It featured a few animals and such novelties as a little booth where people would pay a nickel to see the "spring." They expected

One of Johnny's favorite gandies was Jim Headley, here
sporting the injuries from a head-on crash that killed his two
companions. His escape from death earned him the nickname
"the survivor." Courtesy of John and Barbara Bacich.

to see artesian water spurting from the parched Alabama clay. Instead, they saw an old metal bedspring. Those kinds of sucker attractions don't go over well for very long. Perhaps that's why Headley left Alabama and headed north to join the other lost souls in a cold and distant Skid Row, where Johnny dried him out enough that he could be put to work.

Most of the time, as he sat in his chair looking at the photographs, one by one, I heard Johnny make a sound, like he was reaching in the dark for a cord that he thought would turn on the light but just ended up scooping air. For the most part, he had no idea who these guys were. I had wanted to believe every three-by-five-inch photo would release a fully formed story, as if each image of a face were a key that fit the lock on an individual compartment in Johnny's ninety-year-old brain. The door would open and out would come the ghost of the gandy, who would introduce himself, act out his own poignant skit, and then take a bow, making way for the ghost in the next drawer.

But in Johnny's mind and everywhere else, the men of Minneapolis's Skid Row survive only in fragments. They did not write memoirs, consent to large-group photographs, or participate in long oral history interviews now stored at the library. Even in Johnny's Skid Row movies, they are silent, though the herky-jerky, slightly sped-up footage shows their mouths moving, sometimes in laughter, sometimes in anger. The Bell & Howell camera wasn't equipped for sound, so the voices of Whitey and Doc and the old Republican and Santa Claus and the guy who climbed on roofs and the rest of those long-dead characters were never recorded. Johnny had to speak for his gandies, and even he couldn't remember the names of most of them.

The photographs that others took have the same problem. The craggy faces and missing limbs and baggy clothes of the Gateway bums were fascinating to the art photographers at the University of Minnesota, who had them pose in doorways among discarded liquor bottles or pictured them with a spoon of mission gruel suspended in their mouths. We see the backs of heads in the photos of the grand demolition, watching the wrecking ball tear through masonry walls so easily it looks as if they're made of clay. The one thing that always seems to be missing is their names, and if I was trying to do anything with this project, I wanted to retrieve as many as I could.

I got many explanations for why Johnny took pictures of his men, depending on when I asked him. He needed a mug shot for debt collection purposes so it would be easier to track the guys down when they ran out on their rent or liquor bills. Sometimes the FBI or the local cops would ask to see them, if they were looking for a fugitive, or maybe a corpse had surfaced in the Mississippi and at some point the man may have been a guest at the Victor Hotel. I have my own theory. Looking at how Johnny pinned them up on the wall of his office, he probably felt as if they had joined his extended family. He had sat them down in his office and talked to them, found out how they washed up in Minneapolis. He took them in, enrolling them in the Bacich room, board, and booze program, then he had captured their likenesses, and now they belonged to him.

He called them gandies. It's short for gandy dancers, a slang term for railroad workers, and nobody really knows where it came from. The Victor Hotel had a larger number of current and former railroad workers than any other flophouse in the central Gateway in 1958, so many of Johnny's gandies had actually driven spikes, hauled crossties, and dragged rails, although by the time he knew them many of the men collected the railroad pension that everyone called the "rocking chair." Many came from far away, all the way from the South, and others only traveled maybe a mile, like the fellow who got tired of the squalling and yelling in his home at Twenty-Sixth Avenue and Twenty-Sixth Street so he walked out the door. He got a cubicle at the Victor, signed on to the railroad, and gave up on his family, forever.

These men were the last generation of the seasonal workers who had populated the city for the better part of a century. Given how much the city leaders spent to get rid of them, it's perhaps fitting that their names have likewise been virtually wiped from the record. They were known broadly as Skid Rowers, transients, deviants, winos, vagrants, hoboes. Mostly, anyone who visited or lived elsewhere in the city recognized the bums on Washington Avenue as permanent characters in Minneapolis's civic drama. One of my wife's uncles recalls cruising down the avenue in the 1950s just to gawk at the sidewalk antics of the men, ambling, scuffling, staggering, or just lying passed out. The sociologists and planners paid more earnest attention, studying their habits so closely that they could predict a panhandler's script as he worked his way down the sidewalk. Perhaps the strangest description of all, though, was "homeless." Men who had lived in the same cubicle for thirty years could not claim it as a home. According to the mores of the 1950s, no rational person would choose to live in such conditions. It was also common practice to make a homeless person move along. In fact, it was viewed as doing them a favor.

The ideal residential landscape of the 1950s was a row of ramblers and green lawns on a tidy street where stay-at-home moms raised children while the dads were off at work. The Gateway was everything those neighborhoods were not: urban, male, idle, and old. A 1952 city report concluded that the denizens of the Gateway were making a bad impression on visitors and the fairer sex: "The removal of these unsightly men from the streets and particularly from the alleys would add to the feeling of security and safety of ladies and strangers in the city." The following year, Frank Murray of the *Minneapolis Star* decided it was the three thousand or so people who lived in the heart of the city who were the interlopers. "Who are these strangers within our Gateway?" his 1953 article began. "Where do they come from? Why are they here? What can be done about them?" His words showed just how far the city had distanced itself from its roots, so that most Minneapolitans would barely recognize the kinds of people who had lived there as long as, and longer than, just about anybody else.

Murray described seeing men "leaning elbows on parking meters, and chatting with a circle of friends like women over a picket fence." Lovald observed five years later: "During the daytime, Washington Avenue's sidewalks, curb-stones, parking meters and storefronts accommodate, in greatest number, elderly men standing in clusters or walking alone." He went on: "Many of them are congested in small groups, some leaning against parking meters, others sitting on the fenders of parked cars or on the curb. A few, in advanced stages of intoxication, will be moving along very slowly talking to themselves."

In July 1958, the city commissioned the University of Minnesota's Department of Sociology to help them understand the scope of the problem. The sociologists and a small army of graduate students, including Lovald, attempted to draw some lines around the problem. They surveyed the neighborhood that month and learned that there were 2,905 people living in the "relocation area." Ninety-six percent were white men. Only 125 or so were women. These men were old, too. More than half had never married. Sixty percent were unemployed. Two-thirds lived on some kind of public assistance. The ratio of men to available toilets was 10 to 1. For the 1950s, this was the height of deviance.

A resident of Skid Row was easy to recognize. Lovald offered a guide to their fashion no-nos, such as the "disharmony of a blue double-breasted suit coat and a pair of green trousers." By the late 1950s, double-breasted suits were clearly out of style, so that meant they were widely available in the secondhand clothing stores of the Gateway. One store alone had 4,700 men's suits. If the clothes didn't give away a Skid Rower, however, his mouth would. "Perhaps the single most distinguishing mark of the homeless man today is his teeth," Lovald wrote. "If they are not absent, or in short supply, they are most likely to be extremely yellow and tobacco stained." Brushing one's teeth was not a common habit in the flophouses. The edentulous learned to live without. "An old man without a tooth in his head was asked, since he was eligible for medical benefits, why he did not investigate the possibility of getting some false teeth. The nature of his reply indicated he was afraid he would swallow them or that if he took them out during the evening, they would be stolen."

Indeed, thievery was so widespread that the gandy dancers must have felt everything was owned in common. If anyone was drunk or foolish enough to leave something around, however worthless it seemed, that item was clearly ready for new ownership. Jack Kerr, a resident of the Oslo Hotel at 113½ South Washington, decided one warm night to hang his pants on his bedpost next to an open window. He awoke to find the pants outside on the fire escape, minus the $4.40 he had in the pockets. One of the saddest scenes in Johnny's movie is the image of a destitute fellow, sitting on the curb after being tossed out of his home. While he contemplates what must have been the latest in a lifetime of bad shakes, his suitcase has broken open on sidewalk, and the gandy dancers are helping themselves to the few possessions therein, like pigeons on spilled popcorn. "Oh shit, if you fell asleep anywhere, you'd be lucky if you had any clothes on at all when you woke up," Johnny told me.

Virtually every one of his employees stole from him, and his bar was full of professional shoplifters, or boosters, so he felt he had no choice but to let the kleptoculture work for him. One of the most memorable boosters was an old guy, maybe seventy-five years old, who hailed from the prairie of southwestern Minnesota and dressed the part. His usual garb was a pair of very baggy overalls with straps over his shoulders. These were no ordinary overalls. He had sewn plastic down by the pant cuffs, in effect turning his clothing into a roomy receptacle for contraband. And he steal he did, from every department store he walked into. "You could throw anything down there, and it wouldn't go all the way through," Johnny told me. "He would steal toasters, portable radios, records, you name it. If you needed something, you'd tell him and he'd have it that evening." Alas, no one was safe from the habits of the elderly booster. "The son of a bitch, I caught him stealing in my store," Johnny said. Somehow, it still surprised him, fifty years later. "He had a whole quart of whiskey down in his thing. I said, 'I've been good to you, treated you decent, and now you're stealing from me.' He said, 'A thief's a thief.'"

Jim Wiggins, who worked at the Senate Bar and Café two doors down from Johnny's Sourdough Bar, told an interviewer in 1998 about the booster who served as his bar's private haberdasher. The thief took orders for shirts or anything else you needed for your wardrobe. "He was very well dressed, with a big coat. I didn't know he was stealing them at first. I'd get Arrow shirts for a buck and a half." Johnny's sartorial score was a charcoal-gray Hickey Freeman suit, delivered to him by a booster who got his dimensions first and then secured the goods. He knew another guy named Callahan, who had a partner, and the two would travel to small towns and visit the little department stores that used to operate on every Main Street. They would ask for a whole bunch of shirts, and once the merchandise, still wrapped, was piled on the counter, they would ask the clerk for a shirt on the very top shelf. That meant the clerk had to move the ladder over and climb up to get it. Quick as a flash, Callahan's buddy would grab a bunch of shirts from the pile and slide them into a box he was carrying, the side conveniently sliced open. Callahan would buy a shirt or two, and then they would leave. Soon one of them would come back, to return all the shirts, stolen and purchased, and collect the refund. Johnny knew female boosters, too. One of them wore a stiff skirt and could fit a full suit between her legs and waddle out of a store without being noticed. Another one had a special coat with twelve pockets sewn on the inside. She could fit six, eight, ten pints of whiskey in her coat, which must have been heavy when she hoofed it down the sidewalk.

Down on Skid Row, everyone may have been a thief, as Johnny said, but they were just as likely to share whatever bounty they had, particularly when it came to booze. Nobody had anything for very long, so you might as well spend it now and bring your friends along for the ride. There was one guy who rang the big drinks-on-me bell at the Sourdough Bar just about every day. Johnny didn't remember his real name, but that didn't matter, because his nickname, Needles, was all you needed to know. He told people he was a disabled World War II veteran, but he had more than his story to sell. He borrowed twenty bucks from somebody to buy a big carton of pins and needles, maybe two thousand packs in all, at a penny apiece. Then he would sell them on the sidewalk at a substantial markup to women on their way home after leaving the Gateway's tailor shops. He was Skid Row's equivalent of the little orphan girl standing barefoot in the snow, selling pencils from a cup. One time Johnny Rex made a bet that he couldn't make 50 dollars. Three hours later, Needles came back with 150 bucks. And everybody drank free.

The longer I knew Johnny, the more scraps of his Skid Row days would float to the surface, but in strange ways. One time, he sent me a handwritten note on a piece of notepad paper from the Fairfield Inn. "I'd bring food, nice chicken sandwiches etc free, but they were too sick to eat. I had army officers, doctors, businessmen, one who quoted poetry and all walks of life. Very few lived beyond their fif-

Johnny named his bar after his brother-in-law's establishment in Alaska. That joint is still in operation. Courtesy of John and Barbara Bacich.

ties. Alcoholism wasn't known until A.A. in the late 1950s!" He signed it, "J Rex." Another day I got a letter from him in a standard envelope. I unfolded the paper, and unfolded it again, until it was its full eleven by seventeen inches. At the top of the page, Johnny had placed his old business card.

> Ketchican, Alaska and Minneapolis, Minnesota
> Sour Dough Bar
> 34 South Washington Avenue
> John Bacich

The rest was a photocopy of a poem typed on a manual typewriter, titled "THE TRAMP."

My itchen feet have carried me over mountain top and hill
They are always taking off some where they are never standing still
I just gotta keep amoven or I know I'm gonna bust
I have contracted that disease of tramps they call the wanderlust.

Tho I do a lot of traveling I don't go in for fancy style
It's just any way to get there just to make another mile.
I've traveled in the summer time, and I've traveled in the fall,
And I've made some trips in winter that all too well I recall.

THE GANDIES

Now I've traveled in the sun shine in a snow storm or the rain
And I cook my grub in tin cans while I'm waiten for a train.
Now these railroad bulls keep tellen me I gotta pay a fare
to go from here to there but it's plain again my principles to give
them any fare.

Now I've topped sugar beets in Montana and picked spuds
in Idaho.
But worken don't agree with me just why I'll never know.
I guess I'll have an allergy to work just as long as I can beg.
Some times I pretend I've got a crippled back or perhaps a gimpy leg.

I bum the butcher and the baker and a vegetable stand or two
And usually I can get enough to cook me up a real good
mulligan stew.
Then I see some prosperous looken feller and I lay it on the line
And I always seem to get some cash to buy a jug of wine.

If we tramps get into Heaven like the preachers say we do,
Then I hope that I'll be goen there when my life on Earth is through.
I'll put the bum on old Saint Peter when I come in through the gate,
I'll just tell him I'm real hungry it's a week now since I ate.

I'll put the bum on some rich angel so I'll get a jug of wine
You can bet in 15 minutes I'll be feelin pretty fine.
I'll cook a real big mulligan stew and I'll sleep out in the park
I'll go travelin up in Heaven just a playen on my harp.

It's signed at the bottom, "Leif G. Erickson," and then there's an address that looks like 2306 [illegible] Mpls.

The next time I saw John, I asked him where the poem came from.
I was expecting quite a story. Nope. "I don't know where I found it.
That's a good question." He had no memory of Mr. Erickson, who will
remain a minor poet in the largely forgotten tradition of hobo verse.

One thing I noticed about Johnny's memory was his vivid recollection of every violent confrontation between his gandies, and espe-

cially every time he had to enforce his authority with his fists. This was not unique to him. In this respect, Keith Lovald, the sociologist, hit it on the head, so to speak: "A frequent conversation filled with reminiscences heard among the Gateway's oldsters concerns physical combat ('I remember when I beat the hell out of'). A particularly noteworthy fight will be discussed for days in the lobbies and in the bars. The fight has significance beyond its mere spectator appeal. It unifies the community." Johnny remembers one confrontation that broke out in a cubicle in the Victor Hotel. A strapping young man with bulging biceps, dressed all in khaki, checked in. John had a feeling that the guy didn't want to spend his nights alone, so he emphatically conveyed one of the main house rules: no women in the hotel. The only females allowed were the ones printed on paper and pinned to the walls. Sure enough, though, the guy got to drinking for a couple of days and decided that he needed some companionship. Johnny stopped by the cage one night and noticed that Mr. Khaki wasn't alone. Sitting on his bed, naked from the waist up, sat an extremely well-endowed young woman ("tits that wouldn't quit," was Johnny's description). This made John angry, so he took a roundhouse swing at the guest, who ducked. Johnny Rex's fist connected with the tin corduroy wall of the cubicle. That's what he remembered most from that encounter: the feeling of punching hard metal. John may have missed the mark that day, but he told me that story so many times because he wanted to show the lengths to which he would go to enforce the code of the Victor. Its strange equilibrium could endure plenty of drunken benders and fistfights and even an occasional corpse, but it could not abide a sexual liaison.

Johnny said the gandies had a competition to see which one could knock him off his feet. Only one guy ever did, and his name was Jungle Jim. Johnny Rex was looking for Nick Fiestal, one of the two nose pullers, a resident of the Victor Hotel, and one of his best workers. Nick had been arrested for something, and when he got out of jail, he didn't come back to the hotel for his shift. John heard that Nick had been sleeping underneath the Third Avenue Bridge, in the midst of the "jungle." Every Skid Row had its jungle, the patch of woods surrounding the railroad tracks, which served as a leafy place to sober up for a few days away from the police. It was also a convenient campground for those who might have to leave in a hurry. In Minneapolis the jungle spread across both sides of the Mississippi River. On the west bank it provided cover for those jumping trains leaving the Great Northern Depot. On the east bank, where James J. Hill's monumental Stone Arch Bridge met the shore, the jungle offered clear springwater, flowing out of the limestone, and caves for shelter. The jungle was freedom, a place where a man could catch a fish and boil it up in a "gunboat"—a large metal canister repurposed as a cooking pot—over an open flame without molestation from the authorities.

When he went in search of Nick, Johnny was wearing a suit for some important meeting that day. He must have looked a sight, this businessman crossing the railroad tracks and scrambling down the steep brushy slope to the Mississippi River. He looked in the usual hiding places and campsites, but Nick was nowhere to be found. John trudged back through the woods, frustrated and in a hurry. This time, he came across Polack Wally and Jungle Jim, waiting by the tracks. Jim made a smart comment, Johnny gave it right back to him, and the next thing they knew, they were squaring off, fists up, the hobo versus the suit. Jim's wrists were thick, and his hands were fast. "I have to get to you in a hurry, before you get me," John said. "You ain't going to get to me," Jim said, and smashed Johnny in the face and jabbed him in the side. The punch opened a cut over Johnny's eye, and his chest hurt something awful. The fight was over fast, and somehow Johnny got away. He went to see his doctor, who told him he had three cracked ribs under his blazer.

The next morning, Johnny saw Polack Wally. "Where's Jungle Jim?"

"He's in Chicago," Wally said. "I tried to tell you. He fought semi-pro for ten years. He was an undefeated navy champion."

Jim knew Johnny might try to have him arrested, so he had hopped a freight train and got out of town fast. But knowing that a bona fide boxer, not just an average hobo, had bested him must have softened Johnny's determination for revenge.

Johnny also traveled to Chicago all the time, but in a comfortable seat on an airplane, not on the hard floor of a boxcar. When the gandies owed him money and hopped the rails instead of paying their debts, Johnny figured out how to make himself whole. The unemployment checks were mailed to his hotel, so all he had to do was take the checks with him, find the gandy dancer in some Chicago flophouse, get his signature, and go home. He could cash the check and keep the money. About a month after his beating on the railroad tracks, Johnny saw Jungle Jim on the street in Chicago. Jim turned to run, but Johnny called out, "Don't worry, I won't turn you in." "Can you at least buy me a drink?" Jim asked. Johnny felt a wave of generosity toward the man who had knocked him down but still knew who was boss. "I'll buy you two drinks," he said.

Johnny's film shows that fisticuffs were a regular pastime on the streets of Skid Row. There's as much pummeling and gore as there is laughter and merrymaking. Two guys in shirtsleeves box in an alley, out for blood. Another guy crawls out from under a stoop, his face a swollen bloody pulp, and drinks compulsively from a pint bottle, trying to kill the pain. Another man sits cross-legged on the sidewalk, dejectedly looking at the ground. His face looks as if it has been rammed repeatedly into a post, and the next frame shows the cops putting him into a car headed for General Hospital.

It wasn't all about violence. Love would break out among the men as well, or at least, lust. "Homosexuality—especially among tramps—and visits to prostitutes were the most prevalent forms" of sex, Lovald wrote. The going rate for a Gateway prostitute was five bucks. In fact, plenty of the men were gay, but "no attempt was made to discover the frequency of its incidence." In the 1950s, there were some places even sociologists were afraid to go. None of this seemed to faze Johnny, who had this to say about the group of gay men who gathered at the Sourdough most mornings. "If you don't like them, just leave them alone." This was no small thing. Gay people in 1950s Minneapolis were regularly beaten up and robbed, and they could expect the same rough treatment from the cops if they tried to complain about it. In Johnny's film, a skinny old man does a gyrating-hip dance for the camera. That was Doc, "one of the gays," Johnny says, in his matter-of-fact way. "The old man of the gays." Perhaps the sidewalks of Skid Row were one place Doc felt comfortable performing his dance

Doc was "the old man of the gays" and benefited from Johnny's tolerant attitude toward gay men frequenting his bar at a time when they were unwelcome at most Minneapolis establishments. From the film *Skidrow*. Courtesy of John and Barbara Bacich.

routine. The Dugout Bar, a few blocks from the Sourdough at Second Avenue and Third Street, was also a gathering place for working-class gay men, though lesbians were discouraged from socializing in bars by the city's old blue law that prohibited unescorted women in saloons.

While the Gateway had some of the few relatively safe gay spaces in Minneapolis, the city had no intention of tolerating female sex workers. In the mid-1950s, Skid Row was host to a new scourge that gave city leaders another reason to hate the place. Now it was an incubator of gonorrhea and syphilis, spread by prostitutes who frequented the dingy bars and flophouses. The *Minneapolis Star* blamed it on penicillin, because the drug enabled those women to banish the disease long enough to carry on their work. At two dollars a shot, the drug allowed the "blowzy creatures" to keep "plying their trade." "Prostitutes are diseased one day and 'cured' the next; syphilis and gonorrhea no longer hold the economic and health terrors they once did," the newspaper lamented. The Minneapolis Police Morals Squad targeted these "undesirable persons" with raids on Gateway bars in January 1958. "We want to show this kind of woman that the morals squad knows they are in town," declared Dan Graff, head of the squad. The working women corralled in these raids were often given the option to avoid jail by leaving town and promising not to return. When modern-day banishment failed to curb the trouble, the city went after the venues themselves.

The city's new health director was determined to end the "revolving door of venereal disease and sexual vice." Dr. Karl Lundeberg was a preacher's son and a longtime disease fighter who spent most of his career in the Army. In World War II, his principal enemies were the tropical diseases sickening GIs from Guadalcanal to North Africa. His success elevated Lundeberg to the rank of lieutenant colonel, and he looked the part, with spectacles, an erect bearing, and a pipe between his lips. In Minneapolis, the colonel's enemies were chancres and painful urination and the even more sinister symptoms of VD, which seemed to be spreading throughout the city, despite campaigns against gonorrhea and syphilis since the 1940s. Lundeberg used the language of crime to describe health code violations. Drunks and prostitutes committed "sanitary offenses," and it was the health department's job to practice "sanitary surveillance": aggressive enforcement of health standards at restaurants, bars, and hotels. In Lundeberg's view, Skid Row sustained a cycle of disease. "The drunk who throws empty bottles in the street or alley, urinates, vomits, and expectorates indiscriminately will remain unless checked by some means," he wrote. "Prostitutes and female 'bar flies' attract patronage to some of these drinking places and no doubt contribute to excessive drinking, to venereal disease, and to other disorders that constitute the hallmarks of skidrow and social blight."

In 1958, any General Hospital patient with suspicious discharges

George Johnson planted a kiss on an unknown woman while
other gandies, including Jim Shelley *(second from left)* and Jim
Headley *(third from left)* looked on. They were gathered in
Rex Liquors, Johnny's off-sale at 201 Nicollet Avenue South.
Courtesy of John and Barbara Bacich.

or burning sensations "down below" faced sensitive questions from public health workers about the donor of these unwanted gifts. Lundeberg soon narrowed down the "places of encounter" to a single block of Washington Avenue, smack dab in the middle of Skid Row. The establishments included the Sourdough Bar, which Johnny was well aware served as a gathering place for prostitutes who spent their off-hours drinking cups of coffee and comparing notes. Still, when he found out that Dr. Lundeberg had the Sourdough in his crosshairs, Johnny got on the horn with Wolinski, his friend on the city council, to find out why. It turned out that a student at DeLaSalle High School ("He was a DeLaSalle punk. A punk!") blamed his syphilitic misery on the woman he had hired after meeting her at the Sourdough. Dr. Lundeberg thought he had enough evidence of a public health menace for the city to pull the plug on Johnny's bar. Wolinski and Johnny weren't going to let that happen without a fight. The alderman set up a meeting with Lundeberg, and Johnny brought along his lawyer, Scoop Lohmann. Though he made officer late in the war, John Bacich remained an enlisted man at heart. He felt a special antipathy toward the colonel, who in John's opinion acted as if he had his rank tattooed on his belly. Dr. Lundeberg could probably feel Johnny's loathing, but he had a job to do, and he told everyone about the infected high school kid and how allowing places like the Sourdough to stay in operation would threaten the city's future with the clap. Wolinski piped up. Fine, he said; then Roosevelt, Washburn, Central, West, North, South, and every other high school in Minneapolis should be closed, because there was more syphilis in those places than on Skid Row. "That was the end of it," Johnny told me, and whether Dr. Lundeberg was persuaded, or just intimidated by the alderman, no one will ever know. But John was learning how to get things done in Minneapolis. Maybe he had some business sense after all. That October, the health director stood up in front of the city council and urged it to shut down the licenses of three disease-spreading establishments: the 24 Bar, the Gay Nineties, and the Senate Hotel. They formed a ring around the Sourdough, but Johnny's saloon remained untouched, for the moment.

The same month Dr. Lundeberg warned of the VD menace, a

Elmer Kistler sits in his cubicle at the Beacon Hotel,
40 Washington Avenue South, a few doors down from the
Sourdough, in 1958. Kistler was an odd-jobs man from Kansas
City who knew he had to leave the Beacon but hoped he would
not lose the companionship he had found in the Gateway.
Photograph by Larry Schreiber, *Minneapolis Star Tribune*.
Courtesy of the Minnesota Historical Society.

Minneapolis Star reporter named Martin Merrick canvassed the flop-houses and buttonholed residents about the city's plans to evict them in the name of blight clearance. Amazingly, in contrast to other journalists during the period, Merrick actually did some reporting, instead of writing about the guys as if they were urban wildlife. For once, the men of Skid Row were depicted not as disease carriers or drunken sociopaths or skulking thieves, but as actual human beings.

At the Beacon Hotel, Merrick met Elmer Kistler, a relatively young (forty-three) "odd-jobs man" who had left Kansas City when he was orphaned at age fourteen. He had lived in Minneapolis for twenty-two years. Kistler knew his $3.50-a-week room at the Beacon Hotel, just a few doors down from the Sourdough, was destined for destruction. "I don't mind where I live if I can have companionship," he told Merrick. "There are some darn nice fellows around here." He took a seat on his bed while a newspaper photographer took his picture. He was neatly dressed, with a collared shirt tucked into slacks, and he sat with his hands loosely clasped between his knees, shoulders slightly hunched, his face somber, his eyes looking slightly away from the camera, as if trying to glimpse a life outside those corrugated tin walls. The photograph is captioned: "Not much room maybe, but he likes it there."

Elmer Kistler died in 1967, ten days short of his fifty-third birthday. He is buried in the National Cemetery at Fort Snelling, just down the river from downtown. Quite a few gandies are there, some burial expenses having been paid out of the wallet of John Bacich.

A block away from the Beacon, Pioneer Hotel proprietor Charlie Arnold boasted to Merrick that his tenants included "many fine old gentlemen." Their statements to the reporter seemed to bear this out: Oscar Elmquist, sixty-nine years old, said, "If they tore this building down, I suppose I'll have to move, but I hope they put up a new Skid Row before they move us out. We can't live in a vacant lot." Adolph Karlsson chimed in, saying he was agreeable to relocating "if we can have another place where men like myself can stay and have companionship. When a man reaches middle age and he can't get a steady job, he needs a place where he can get a cheap room and cheap meals."

John Ladzikowski called himself Mr. Skid Row, and here he addressed a hearing of the Minneapolis Housing and Redevelopment Authority in December 1958. He warned that if they were expelled from the Gateway, the gandy dancers might spread to the suburbs. Ladzikowski made a short-lived effort to organize his neighborhood, to no avail. Photograph by Charles Brill, *Minneapolis Star Tribune*. Courtesy of the Minnesota Historical Society.

At the Harbor Light mission, Merrick met a self-described "old drunkard" named Orlin Gudmundson and a "retired drinker" named Bert Kingery, who claimed that God had saved him from the bottle. He subscribed to the company line on Gateway redevelopment. "No matter what it is, it's going to be better. Knocking down Skid Row is the best thing that ever happened to this town."

These men seemed to have embraced passivity: the end of their world was nigh, and there was nothing a broken-down railroad man could do about it. Martin Merrick's story left little doubt that Skid Row was no match when the forces of slum clearance were finally brought to bear. The unsightly men, for so long portrayed as a permanent gang of ruffians occupying the good city, would blow away like scraps of newspaper on the sidewalk. Those who rose up in vain to try to stop the wrecking balls were typically the business owners and defenders of the Metropolitan Building, an architectural landmark that had the misfortune of occupying the fraying edge between respectable downtown Minneapolis and the rotten old core. Advocates for the three thousand or so human beings who lived in that area were hard to find. Still, one guy, a gandy who lived across the street from Johnny Rex's hotel, showed up at the eleventh hour in a valiant effort to do his civic duty and represent his hapless peers.

At a public hearing in December 1958, that man came to the microphone to speak to the members of the city's Housing and Redevelopment Authority. He introduced himself as John Ladzikowski and said he lived at 26 South Second Street. He was heavyset, clean-shaven, fifty-nine years old, with close-cropped blond hair and small, delicate ears. He wore a jacket over a collared shirt. His message: please make up your minds about what you're going to do with us.

"I'm one of the Mr. Skid Rows. We don't really want to be in your area, but something's got to be done. There's a lot of land where we can go and live and breathe. If you don't want us, we'll go to St. Louis Park, Hopkins, Golden Valley, Bloomington."

That statement must have sent pangs of anxiety through the serious-faced men wearing horn-rimmed glasses, dark suits, and skinny ties. Public support for demolishing Skid Row was dependent on keeping this blight from cropping up somewhere else, and now Mr. Skid Row was invoking the specter of single alcoholics, loafers, drifters, sexual deviants, and nut jobs marching into suburban rambler country.

The alderman for the ward, H. P. Christensen, offered some conciliatory words about Ladzikowski and his fellow residents. Christensen seemed to understand why this supposedly abnormal community had lasted as long as it did: "We don't want to hurt anyone. We want to do a good job of relocating people," the alderman said. "These people have to be cared for. Many have raised a family. In their day they were good honest laborers. When you get old and your children leave you, that's a lonely life. Many of these people need the companionship they get together."

Over the next year, Mr. Skid Row kept showing up at meetings about the redevelopment, and then at meetings and hearings about other matters. He commented about a proposal to eliminate the elected park and library boards. He weighed in on the city charter. He saw it all through the lens of his own fate, now a priority of the city fathers. That year, he tried valiantly to organize his fellow Skid Rowers. In early 1959, he wrote in a widely circulated handbill:

Attention—This concerns you!

If you live on skid row and are 65 years old
and are on social security or state disability
This concerns you.

You have been on trial and were found guilty
as the result of two legal notifications published
in the daily newspapers January 1, 1959,
The city council condemned you to spend the
rest of your life in an area extending from Hennepin
Avenue to the M. & St. L. tracks, by Traffic
Street North and the alley of Washington Avenue
through Third Street North,
This area is a business area. It's noisy,
dusty, filled with dust and auto gas fumes.

If you don't want to live in a dormitory the
rest of your life, being told when to get up and
when to go to bed, what time to eat, and take an
ear beating every night and twice on Sunday then
raise your voice in protest,
Let's all meet on the ground floor of the
city hall on Third Street South, January 19, at
7:15 p.m. Last time I stood alone. I need your
help on this now,

John Ladzikowski
Mr. Skid Row
26 South Second Street
Minneapolis, Minn.

History does not record whether Mr. Skid Row's organizational efforts bore fruit, so he decided to move on his own. By September 1959,
he is listed as the only one of ninety persons who relocated on his own
accord, not because his hotel was bought and emptied. He was said
to have moved to north Minneapolis, but it may not have been far
north. He listed his address as 226 North Washington Avenue, only
about four blocks from his old home and right in the midst of the foul
air of the Warehouse District. After his move, he vanishes from the
news accounts. The death certificate for John Ladzikowski indicates
he died barely a year later, on January 7, 1961, in Hennepin County.
He was only sixty.

RING IN THE BOOZE

"My dad always used to say, when you get
them drunk, you just don't discard them.
And he was very compassionate that way."
—Johnny Rex

The Sourdough Bar's first customers of the day gathered on the
sidewalk just before 8 a.m. Often twenty or twenty-five of them
would queue up in the quiet of the morning, the previous night's debauchery brought to mind only by a sour smell and broken glass in
the gutter, a shoeless figure asleep in a doorway. Those who were
upright formed a line of suffering on Washington Avenue, heads
pounding, stomachs heaving, hands shaking, probably not talking
much as they waited under the storefront's colossal foaming beer
glass and the immense 10, the never-changing price of a beer. In the
driving snow or pissing rain, the morning ritual endured, and when
the clock on city hall struck eight and the door swung open, the alcoholics shambled in. They were rewarded with the early bird special:
a five-cent glass of muscatel, the kind of breakfast that took the edge
off their pain and allowed them to begin another day on a journey
down the boozy river to oblivion.

The five-cent policy was the brainchild of the proprietor, Johnny
Rex. Even though he was in control of his urges and could stop after
a drink or two, the sight of people with brutal hangovers always

Johnny and one of his favorite habitués of the Sourdough, "Moon Face Mary Ann." "She was one of the nicest gals I've ever known. She had a personality like crazy. She would come in at eight o'clock and wouldn't leave until one in the morning." Photographer unknown. Courtesy of John and Barbara Bacich.

brought out his charitable side. He hated to see them so ill when he knew he had the means to relieve their agony, means that were more immediate and reliable than those of the Harvest Field Mission or the Minnesota State Employment Service just across the alley from the Sourdough's back door. It wasn't a bad business model, either, and Johnny was never one to look away from opportunity. When they're sick, they're sick, he reasoned, and he had the treatment. The other shopkeepers and bar owners on the block would complain about the morning sidewalk spectacle and the five-cent eye-openers, but they always complained because Johnny had figured out a way to under-price them and still make a profit. In his view, he was taking care of those guys. He didn't jackroll them. He didn't get them drunk and steal from them. He treated them like family, with that signature Bacich generosity.

He got that from his father, the benevolent despot who reigned over his soused minions at the long-forgotten Palimar Bar of Oliver, Wisconsin. Take care of your customers, even as you get them hammered. Don't just toss them in the gutter. Such was the peculiar psychology of Skid Row, where the barkeeps were the caretakers. "The bartender acts as a kind of guardian to many of his customers, seeing that they get home when they are drunk, protecting them from police and jackrollers, and sometimes extending them credit," wrote sociologist Sam Wallace, who impersonated a Gateway drunk for his field research. Johnny Rex probably took it as far as anybody, owning the Skid Row trifecta of a liquor store, bar, and flophouse, where he would comp anybody a drink because he knew they'd always be back.

This support network for heavy drinkers anguished those who were concerned about the city's image, but it revealed something fundamental about the place. Minneapolis has always had a tortured relationship with the bottle. From its earliest days as a frontier boomtown built on timber and grain, its New England–born plutocrats alternately profited from and fretted over the city's growing reputation as a place where lumberjacks, farmers, and railroad workers could spend their cash on vices in short supply outstate. As the city attracted legions of Scandinavians, they brought with them a fondness for brännvin, but also a culture of temperance. In 1884 the

Drinkers at the Valhalla Bar and Cafe, 105 Washington Avenue
South, 1960. The special, posted above the bar: hot brandy,
Mohawk 5 Star California Finest, thirty-five cents for a single,
fifty cents a double. And if you were hungry, you could slide over
a couple of stools to the lunch counter. Courtesy of the City of
Minneapolis.

city drew a line around the downtown, a section of northeast Minneapolis, and a few other places and said no drinks could be served outside those boundaries. Officially termed the Liquor Patrol Limits, the boundaries accomplished several things: They kept legal booze out of the civilized and rational grid of neighborhoods and streetcar suburbs to the south and north. They also ensured nearly a century of municipal corruption, in which control of liquor permits became a cash cow for gangsters and their willing partners in city hall.

Each ward's elected representative had the sole discretion to grant or deny liquor licenses in his area, and this unwritten policy of "aldermanic courtesy" was an invitation to self-dealing and bribery. Johnny had particular antipathy for the long-serving Fourth and Seventh Ward alderman, Romeo Riley, whose campaign motto of "dependable, efficient, honest" was belied by his business practices. Riley's day job was selling cleaning chemicals, and those to whom he granted liquor licenses in his ward made sure to buy Riley's soap to shine their bar floors.

Every major city had its Skid Row, but no other city had geographical liquor limits quite like Minneapolis. Those boundaries turned the Lower Loop into a virtual catchment basin of alcohol, an extraordinary concentration of bottle shops, saloons, beer joints, and ancillary businesses irrigated by muscatel wine, cheap whiskey, Minnesota-brewed beer, and even face lotion and Sterno consumed by the lowest of the low, the "dehorns." In what seemed like a devil's bargain, the rest of the city surrendered the Gateway to the dark kingdom of demon rum.

A 1952 survey found an astonishing sixty-two bars and liquor stores in the Gateway, or the equivalent of one bar for every seventy-nine people who lived there. That number hadn't changed much by 1958. One researcher made the following observation about a similarity in the nineteen liquor stores in the neighborhood: "Nowhere else in Minneapolis is one likely to encounter the question, upon buying a bottle of wine, 'Do you want it opened?'" The wettest block of all was Block 10, bounded by Washington Avenue, Nicollet Avenue, Second Street South, and Marquette Avenue. You could stagger between eight bars and three liquor stores without crossing a street,

In 1955 Alderman Frank Wolinski hoists a map of the
Minneapolis Liquor Patrol Limits, the zone outside of which
liquor could not legally be sold, except for a few mob-controlled
establishments. Wolinski would fight for two decades to
eliminate those limits. Copyright Star Tribune Media Company
LLC. Reprinted with permission.

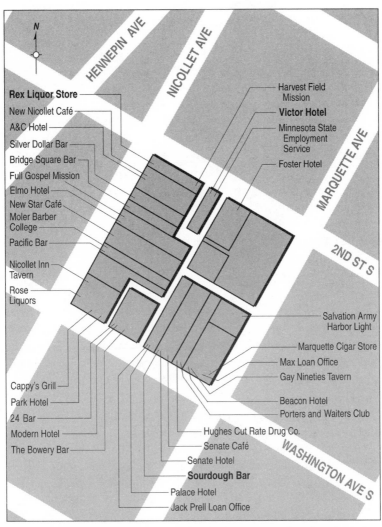

Block 10 was the center of Skid Row, crammed with eight bars, three liquor stores, six lodging houses, three hotels, and a rooming house. It was home to Johnny's three establishments: the Victor Hotel, Rex Liquors, and the Sourdough Bar. Map by Philip Schwartzberg, Meridian Mapping, Minneapolis.

although you might have to lean against the bricks as you rounded the corner. You also had your choice of six lodging houses, three hotels, and a rooming house. You could eat in three restaurants, sell your overcoat or revolver in two pawnshops, save your soul in three missions, and maybe find some hard labor for a day at the employment office.

Johnny Rex's first foray into the liquor business downtown was on the edge of the Gateway. Sometime in the early 1950s Johnny had heard a license was available, and with the help of Frank Wolinski, the alderman who specialized in liquor permit deals, paid $1,500 for it. I always wondered how Johnny was able to get it, given that the city's liquor licensing was almost all controlled by two gangs, one led by a Romanian immigrant named Isadore "Kid Cann" Blumenfeld, and the other by Irish mobster Tommy Banks. The Kefauver Crime Commission labeled Kid Cann "the most outstanding racketeer in Minneapolis," and he dressed the part, once granting an interview to a reporter while dressed in a maroon suit with a canary-yellow shirt. John told me he was good friends with Harry Bloom, Kid Cann's brother. Bloom was less flamboyant but was the brains of the operation, and Johnny would visit with him at Bloom's headquarters, the Lincoln Del pastrami palace in the Minneapolis suburb of St. Louis Park. The truth is, John Bacich's little liquor store didn't pose much of a threat. Bloom and his dangerous brother had no interest in the cheap, low-margin liquor market on Skid Row. The real money lay in thirty-seven liquor establishments outside the old booze boundary. Their licenses were granted just after the repeal of Prohibition, when the city briefly loosened the city's patrol limits. City leaders quickly tightened the limits again, creating a monopoly of on-sale and off-sale alcohol fully under the control of organized crime for twenty years. Those who benefited from this Prohibition-flavored zoning went to great lengths to preserve it. Johnny recalled that every time the legislature went into session, the mobsters who controlled the most profitable liquor outlets would rent three adjoining rooms at a motel across the river from the capital, in Mendota Heights. Two of the rooms were left vacant to discourage eavesdropping. In the middle room, the mobsters would hold court for visiting legislators.

The message to lawmakers was simple: don't mess with the patrol limits. And so they remained unchanged for decades.

Meanwhile, anyone crazy enough to vie for the scraped-together pennies of gandy dancers was not worth a gangster's time. Johnny's first liquor store was basically a hole in the wall in the faded Andrews Hotel building. The Andrews had once been a decent place, but now the hotel bar was known as a place to pick up a floozy. The Fourth Street Cigar Store, whose principal business had nothing to do with tobacco, operated next door. Its proprietor, Joe Wolk, was a bookie, part of the network that made Minneapolis the nation's hub of sports betting. The city had held that distinction since the mid-1930s, after a local gambling entrepreneur, Leo Hirschfield, developed a system of setting odds and point spreads that would be published and distributed to bookies nationwide. Aided by the city's central location and reliable long-distance phone service, Hirschfield's "Minneapolis line" became the authority for millions of bets until the sports betting world moved to Las Vegas in the early 1960s. The Fourth Street Cigar Store's phone would ring constantly with wagers placed from around the country—that is, until the early 1950s, when police hauled away Wolk for tax evasion. Johnny knew Wolk's line of business, but he had no use for it and wanted to make a living at something he thought (wrongly) wouldn't be disrupted by the police. He nailed some old shelving to the wall, lined up the bottles, and stepped behind the register. John's AAA Acorn Liquor Store, 8½ South Fourth Street, promised "prompt speedy service," and its name guaranteed front billing in the phone book. Its slogan was "small but mighty," which could have been a description of Johnny himself. It wasn't long after he opened for business that he came closer to death than at any time since he rolled through France in a tank. One night in 1953, an armed lunatic posing as an army general had opened fire in city hall, and the gun battle spilled out onto Fourth Street. The Minneapolis cops chased the man down the sidewalk, guns blazing, bullets flying everywhere on a busy city street. One of the officers' bullets missed its target, flew into the liquor store, and hit the wall, half an inch from the curls on Johnny's head.

The cop's errant bullet seemed appropriate, in a way, because his

biggest headaches turned out to be the thirsty officers of the Minneapolis Police Department. Since liquor was the currency of the Gateway, the officers expected their share and Johnny had no choice but to oblige. This was the way things worked in Minneapolis, especially in the Gateway, where one retired patrolman told an interviewer it was an unwritten rule that officers assigned to the Skid Row beat wanted no interference from ranking officers, because the businesses they patrolled paid them protection money. Liquid payoffs got even worse around Christmastime, when squad car after squad car would pull up to AAA Acorn and leave with a complimentary fifth of whiskey. One time Johnny made the mistake of handing out two-pound boxes of Fannie Farmer candy instead of the usual booze. The candy cost more, but he might as well have handed out lumps of coal. "They were so goddamned mad that they stood there, they would put tickets on the cars that were stopped there, in the loading zone," he told me. One time, a high-ranking cop pulled up in a squad car and told Johnny that the two bottles of whiskey he had already donated were not enough. He wanted two more, but kindly offered to drive Johnny to his brand-new location (Rex Liquors at 201 Nicollet). Johnny opened the squad door to get in, but there were four cases of whiskey taking up the backseat. So he got to ride in front instead.

Johnny got used to the payoffs. He'd buy stolen suits from boosters in his bar and give them to the police. One time someone sold him a bunch of shotguns and revolvers, origin unknown, out of the trunk of his car, and Johnny bestowed those upon the cops as well. In exchange for Johnny's "gifts," the officers kept an eye on his store. Johnny Rex never forgot that he was at the mercy of the police and the

The California Wine House, 29 Washington Avenue South, sold liquor across the street from the Sourdough Bar. Gateway liquor stores were well known for asking their customers whether they wanted their wine opened on the spot. Courtesy of the City of Minneapolis.

politicians, as that feeling of powerlessness would eventually drive him out of the booze business forever.

For the time being, Johnny was finding success in selling liquor to the largest collection of resident alcoholics for five hundred miles around. He outgrew his cubbyhole in the Andrews Hotel and found a vacant store a few blocks north. The space had been empty for twenty years. Three stories high, with elegant windows and bricks painted white, the building commanded the corner of Nicollet and Second, right across from Gateway Park. Renamed the Rex Liquor Store, the off-sale occupied the choicest location, big storefront windows on both Nicollet and Second and a doorway accessible from either side of the building's corner post. Unfortunately, the previous occupant of the building, a clothing store called the Hub, had built a showcase for suits around the base of the post. This arrangement provided enough cover to be the perfect pissoir for a passerby with an urgent need, and as a result the vestibule smelled uncommonly foul. John got rid of the showcase, cleaned the place up, put in some fairly classy-looking window displays, and lined his shelves with hundreds of bottles of booze. I don't know how many window-shoppers perused the carefully placed bottles of Schenley whiskey, but it had the look of a real liquor store, and some customers would even take their purchases home before uncapping them. Other people could not wait for the store to open. A young man named Frederick Ironeyes broke into Rex Liquors in the middle of a February night in 1959. The police captured the thief a block away and found the loot—three bottles of vodka and three bottles of whiskey—in a trash can at the Pioneer Hotel, directly across the street from the scene of the crime.

Most of the Rex's legitimate customers likely didn't take their bottles far from the store. A favorite drinking spot was the alley behind the liquor store, dubbed "Party Alley" because so much of the imbibing in Skid Row was a social event. The sociologists were fascinated with these open-air gatherings. They called them bottle gangs, which were really no more than clusters of men passing the bottle and taking swigs until it was empty. Bottle gangs were an established social institution with their own rituals and ethical standards. Collecting money for such an event was called the "San Francisco pool." The cost

Rex Liquors dominated the corner of Nicollet and Second Street, but when this picture was taken in 1960 much of the block had already fallen to redevelopment. To the right is Nicollet Avenue, looking south, and in the foreground is Second Street South, looking east, with the Victor Hotel the last building visible to the far left. Courtesy of the City of Minneapolis.

was not too steep: standard price for a half-pint was 30 cents; a full pint, 65 cents (it is not clear why someone wouldn't want to save the nickel by buying two half-pints, but that was the going price recorded by University of Minnesota researchers). A quart was $1.20, and the big gulp, a full gallon, was a mere $4.15. Once a group obtained enough funds, the "baby is born," according to bottle gang argot. Definite taboos: refusing to take a drink for fear of germs, drinking too much on your turn, and, worst of all, taking the mutual bottle fund and disappearing. Solitary drinking was not for drunks, it was for alcoholics—a Skid Row distinction if ever there was one. Decades before mandatory recycling, dead soldiers were typically left on the ground, and the bottles piled so high that there was a well-known puncture hazard posed to any vehicle that tried to ply the Gateway's alleys.

Not everyone wanted to consume liquor alfresco, however. The more civilized drinker could visit a different Gateway bar every morning and still have some left over a month later. Most of them were little joints, a bar on one side, booths on the other—dark, shabby, and notable only for the occasional robbery or violent fracas that made the inside pages of the *Star* or the *Tribune*. Skid Row specialized in "white tile bars," so named because customers "spat in the white tile-lined gutter that ran parallel to the bar and the bartender rinsed it with water every now and then," a scholar of Minneapolis's peculiar liquor history once wrote. The sociology students, in their exhaustive research, determined that at any given time, about a third of the patrons in Gateway bars were visibly drunk. Most bars prohibited mooching, or begging for drinks, but some of them indulged the impecunious inebriate by allowing that behavior in the afternoons. Some let the drinkers build up a tab, to be repaid when their pension checks came in. Then there were saloons that attracted a better-heeled clientele, the so-called dancing bistros such as the Persian Palms.

The Palms, at 111 Washington Avenue South, was probably the most famous bar in the Gateway, and while some remember it with nostalgia, others echo the sentiment of Minneapolis alderman Robert MacGregor: it was "one of the raunchiest operations in town." Its garish storefront promised three floor shows daily, and though a male customer might have trouble getting close to the strippers, he would find himself beset by female customers, the so-called B-girls. "If you were a guy coming up to the bar, before you know it, two girls were on your back. 'Are you going to buy me a drink, honey?'" Johnny recalled. "Everyone wants to be a big shot. 'Yeah, I'll buy you a drink.'" The specialty at the Palms was a split of champagne, enough for two glasses that held less than a pint between them.

A gandy dancer poses inside Rex Liquors. Courtesy of John and Barbara Bacich.

"They would drink so fast, before you could whistle, you'd owe a couple hundred dollars."

The bar had other techniques for separating customers from their money. Johnny recalled one story. After a night of carousing in the big city, the mayor of Elk River settled his three-hundred-dollar bill at the Persian Palms with a check. The Palms bartender pronounced the signature illegible and crumpled up the check. The mayor wrote a second check and left the bar. The first check was retrieved, ironed smooth, and both were cashed. Presiding over this transfer of wealth was the elderly owner, Harry Smull, whose office in the back of the Palms was the headquarters of a sprawling liquor enterprise. Smull was known as the little big guy, small in stature but commanding as many as eight Gateway liquor establishments through a network of relatives. He controlled, at one time or another, the Little Dandy, Old Bowery, Bowery, Frolics, Copper Squirrel, and Saddle bars. Smull was a Russian immigrant who got to know George Bacich in Superior, Wisconsin. Johnny said they also had bootlegging in common. Naturally, Smull took a shine to George's son and invited him to visit regularly in his office at the Palms. Smull liked to keep large quantities of cash on hand. John said he once saw forty thousand dollars in a drawer, and Smull told him he would dip into it when a police officer needed a payoff. Five thugs once took a much larger sum from Smull, after forcing him at gunpoint to open the safe in his office. Smull complained to the police chief, who expressed sympathy about the loss of six hundred grand, but said Smull should keep quiet unless he wanted the FBI to find out the source of his loose cash. Johnny told me it came from "skimming," or squirreling away a percentage of his bars' receipts out of view of the tax man. Smull eventually did get caught up in the city's 1961 liquor license investigation, but like everybody else, he beat the rap.

After moving his liquor store, Johnny had firmly established his empire on the boozy Block 10. Compared to the other businesses around, his must have seemed upscale. Just down the side street he took over the Victor Hotel, at 21½ Second Street South. Then around the corner, at 34 Washington Avenue South, he opened the Sourdough, his pride and joy.

The Sourdough Bar occupied the same building as the Senate Bar, and they were separated only by the narrow doorway leading to the Senate Hotel ("steam heated rooms!"). The Sourdough's brightly painted black-and-yellow storefront noted its namesake in Ketchikan, Alaska, an older establishment run by Johnny's brother-in-law, Wally Kubley. Johnny may have been honorary mayor of Skid Row, but Kubley would go on to become Alaska's actual commerce commissioner. At night, the marquee bulbs sent a rolling wave of luminescence to two arrows pointing down on either side of the front door. The bar's name, and the invocation of its northern twin, gave the Sourdough a frontier feel, harkening back to the wild days of the lumberjack and railroad man "blowing her in" with pockets full of cash. In reality, most of these workers had long ago parked their lives in a fifty-cent-a-night cubicle and the tight little society of one of America's last Skid Rows. The only beer Johnny sold was brewed up the river by the Gluek brothers, who for a time not only controlled a good share of the beer market but also owned dozens of bars. By the 1950s, the big breweries were selling off their "tied houses," so named because they, and their taps, were tied to the brewers. Otto, a jolly fellow with a big German mustache, was Johnny's main contact with the Glueks. Otto rolled 110 to 125 barrels of beer into the Sourdough every month. Gluek would pay a bonus of $700 to $800 to Johnny if he hit the magic number of 125 barrels—an enormous quantity of brew for a bar of its size. Johnny told me that he let this cash bonus trickle down to the gandies as a sort of frequent tippler benefit. But in case I had any illusions that Johnny was an altruist, he also volunteered that his twelve-ounce glasses actually held only eight ounces, because of a clever bump in the bottom. It was something he learned from the Jewish bar owners, he said, speaking only in admiration for their supposed business sense.

I asked Johnny to describe the inside of the Sourdough, and he recalled the long bar, maybe thirty feet long, and then a row of booths upholstered in pink plastic (which was easy to wipe clean). He did not have much decoration, but he did remember the ship's bell, suspended above the bar. Everybody on Washington Avenue knew what it meant when the big bell rang at the Sourdough Bar. "Drinks are on me!" a lucky fellow with enough cash to burn would tell the bartender, and the gesture earned him the privilege of coming behind the bar and grabbing the bell's chain and sending out peals of good tidings. Instantly that gandy's soon-to-be-expended fortune would be shared with the wider drinking community. The sound of the bell reached beyond the long row of stools and the pink booths, out the door onto Washington Avenue, where the knot of craggy-faced men loitered, waiting for the joyful alarm of a foaming glass of Glueks or a shot of cheap whiskey on the house.

All that imbibing created some sanitation challenges. The Sourdough's counterpart in Ketchikan had the advantage of being built on stilts over the water; the tide would wash away all the detritus dropped over the bar's side. No such luck with the Sourdough in Minneapolis or any other Gateway bar. They would have to make do with a trap door, which opened to a chute that swallowed the empty bottles until they spread out, glacier-like, on the floor of the dank basement, to be forgotten until the chute backed up and would accept no more. Richard Palen, an emissary of the Minneapolis Housing and Redevelopment Authority, photographed one of these vile cornucopias. In the basement of the Pioneer Hotel, an arched brick alcove vomited forth a jumbled heap of Gluek's and Hamm's beer cans, Franzia muscatel, something called Gibson's and Half-Half, and a brand of "white port." It is unknown how high this pile would have to get before someone finally hauled the bottles to the dump.

You would not find the Palms' B-girls at the Sourdough, but even without them, a visitor and his fat billfold would be separated within ten minutes, should the fact of the stuffed wallet become known. Johnny was quite frank about what some of his customers did for

Most liquor establishments in Skid Row disposed of their empties on-site through a trap door. The resulting heap spread into the basement. This bottle dump was discovered in the bowels of the building housing the Pioneer Hotel and the Pastime Bar, 125–127 Nicollet Avenue South. Courtesy of the City of Minneapolis.

a living. His bar was a "conglomeration" of bootleggers, muggers, jackrollers, and thieves of all kinds. One of the other habitués of the Sourdough was a short round woman whose great smiling pumpkin of a head earned her the nickname "Moon Face Mary Ann." Johnny remembered her haunting his bar from open to close. She left the bar only to use the toilet, feed the jukebox, or satisfy the intimate needs of male customers in exchange for cash. The only surviving photo of Johnny from that period shows him holding hands with Moon Face; both are smiling for the camera.

Johnny had nothing good to say about the people who worked for him. His bar manager, Joe, was robbing him blind, even though Johnny thought he treated Joe too well for that kind of behavior. He fired him after he caught Joe drinking with his girlfriend in the bar— a serious violation of protocol. After drifting from job to job, Joe later died at a relatively young age while sitting in his car. Johnny seemed to note this fact with a sense of justice—he always remembered how people died, especially when it happened somewhat violently. Whenever the arc of scoundrels' lives bent sharply toward doom, he felt something was right with the world. He had to admit, though, that he saw plenty of good people flame out, and no small number of them lifted a glass off his bar.

Johnny Rex's vertically integrated Skid Row conglomerate of hotel, bar, and liquor store led to some unusual business arrangements. Rather than pay the clerks who worked the desk of the Victor Hotel, he gave them cases of wine to "bootleg." In its post-Prohibition meaning, bootlegging was breaking up a case on the sly and selling the bottles individually at a markup. So the gandies had an added incentive to keep everybody drinking—they made money off it, too.

The disorder unleashed by Skid Row's torrent of booze was one of the most distressing aspects of the Gateway, as far as the rest of the city was concerned. The papers would relate some of the unfortunate incidents. In 1956 a truck driver visiting from Albany, Indiana, met a woman named Janet in the Bowery Bar, a few doors down from the Sourdough, at 26 Washington. She excused herself after lifting four $100 bills and $95 in loose cash from the trucker, and slipped out a back door. A similar fate greeted a Montana trucker who danced with a red-haired temptress at the Old Bowery Bar, 9 North Washington, on a summer night in 1957. She lured him outside, but it was not his body she was after. Her accomplices pummeled the trucker and made off with $390 in cash and $876 in payroll checks, probably requiring some painful conversations between the driver and his boss. In 1956 Vivian Littlesoldier, a twenty-seven-year-old customer at the Silver Dollar Bar, 207 Nicollet Avenue, got into a fight that left her beaten, kicked, and cut with a broken beer bottle. The newspaper reported that when asked by police, "Miss Littlesoldier would offer no explanation for the attack." Any explanation probably would not have made sense to the cops, anyway. In 1959 a patron of the Bridge Square Bar, next door to the Silver Dollar, felt he was up to any challenge. He was a former wrestler who weighed in at 237 pounds and kept his billfold on a chain. It did not deter the five men who accosted him as he left the bar. He punched one of them, got another in a headlock, and bit a third man hard enough to land him in General Hospital. Still, one thief managed to clip the tether on his billfold and get away with twenty bucks.

Most of these bars were low-budget operations that compensated for their lack of atmosphere with cheap drinks. Their names mostly reflected their lack of pretension, with not one but two bars with Bowery in their titles. One place, the Great Lakes Bar, had a different approach. It called itself the "noisiest joint in town" and had some truly unique features, including mannequins placed on toilets as decorations and chairs with electrical leads that the waitresses could use to send "a mild but emphatic current through the body of a patron or patrons," according to one historian.

The criminal justice system played a leading role in sustaining the inebriate culture of the Gateway. In 1957 a full 44 percent of people arrested in the city were Gateway residents, in their own neighborhood; 95 percent of them were busted for drunkenness. They were typically the winos, the muskies, the lushes—the lowest on the teetering Skid Row totem pole. These men were constantly getting in and out of jail, a cycle that for most seemed unbreakable. Macalester College anthropologist James Spradley, studying Seattle's Skid Row in the 1960s, concluded that the dungeon-like conditions of the local

Two Minneapolis police officers escort a Skid Rower into the Black Maria in 1961. Arrests for drunkenness were a key factor in the cycle of dependency and despair that ruled so many men's lives. Photograph by Earl Seubert. Copyright Star Tribune Media Company LLC. Reprinted with permission.

"bucket," and the dehumanizing treatment at the hands of police, destroyed the spirits of the men he called "urban nomads." The criminalization of their vagabond existence amounted to a "life sentence on the installment plan for living by the tramp culture." One of Spradley's main confidants was William Tanner, a Minnesota-born alcoholic whom a cop robbed on Minneapolis's Skid Row. That was one among many misfortunes that followed Tanner from city jail to city jail, from Milwaukee to San Francisco. "After thirty days in jail, you owe yourself a drunk," Tanner wrote in one letter, capturing the peculiar psychology that Spradley used to name his book.

Johnny knew how alcohol could wreck someone's life, and his camera captured both the comic and the ugly. The most indelible scene from his Skid Row movies is the man in overalls draining a quart of wine in one long swallow. Johnny paid him five bucks to do it for the camera, and he did it twice, his throat pulsing with the gushing rotgut, until there was only air. He handed the empty bottle to another gandy and walked off camera in triumph. Another of Johnny's stunts, when he was feeling generous, was putting a case of half-pints of liquor in the alley. He made the men line up against a building and then gave the signal. They raced forward and swarmed all over the carton, like children chasing candy spilled from a piñata. Lanky men tumbled all over each other, a tangle of hands and legs, and then smiled as they came away displaying their prizes, bottles of liquor that probably cost fifty cents.

Injuries, both intentional and accidental, occurred constantly among drunks in the Gateway. The men in Johnny's mug shots often sport black eyes, scrapes, and lacerations, with hazy memories, if any, of their wounds' origins. Johnny recalled one particularly gruesome event across the street from Rex Liquors, on the edge of Gateway Park. By the early 1950s, the park had become the province of broken bottles and wandering men. The once elegant Beaux-Arts comfort station in Gateway Park had already turned into the crumbling and malodorous "piss palace." In 1953 the city tore it down and surrounded the park with a four-foot iron fence topped with spikes, hoping it would keep men off the grass. One day a drunken man tried to leap over the fence. He didn't make it. Johnny was at Rex Liquors when he heard

Johnny paid five bucks for this guy to drain a bottle of wine for his movie camera. "That's a full quart of wine. No fakes." From the film *Skidrow*. Courtesy of John and Barbara Bacich.

the screams. He ran out of the store, crossed Nicollet Avenue, and found the poor fellow hanging from the fence and howling for help. One of his legs was impaled on a fence spike. Johnny and others managed to detach the man, and an ambulance took him away.

Two doors down from Rex Liquors on Nicollet was a beer joint run by a "vicious" woman named Maggie and her husband. Johnny couldn't remember the name of the place when he told me the story. What happened there, though, haunted his memory. Maggie's beer parlor was equipped with a drainpipe that ran from the bar down to the basement. They poured the foam from the beer taps down the pipe, where it collected in a bucket. One enterprising gandy who lived in the Victor Hotel would regularly sneak into the basement and help himself to the bucket's contents. On one of his trips he noticed a plate of hamburger on the basement floor and decided to help himself to that, too. He didn't know that the meat was laced with poison. Maggie kept it there to kill the rats that ran wild through the cracks and crannies of the building. Writhing in agony, the man staggered upstairs and fell over dead. Johnny said Maggie never got in any kind of trouble over it. Death came to Skid Row in strange ways, and the authorities probably figured the men had it coming.

One bad summer night, a man went into a phone booth at the Sourdough and dialed the number of the *Minneapolis Tribune*. The city editor picked up the phone and barked out the four "Ws" of basic reporting. The dialogue that followed was printed, verbatim, in the paper.

"What's the story?" the editor said.

"It's murder," the man said. "I'm going to kill a woman. She was married . . . now she's getting a divorce. I'm going to kill her tonight."

"When?" asked the editor.

"Right now."

"What with?"

"A switchblade."

"Where are you?"

"At the Sourdough Bar, Washington Avenue."

The editor wanted more on the why.

"What have you got against the woman?"

This went on for a bit, and then the editor had the good sense to call the police. But the trouble wasn't at the Sourdough that night. The man walked two blocks to Hennepin Avenue and paid a visit to the Hub Bar, where a forty-seven-year-old woman named Ruby was drinking beer with some friends. The man waited till she stood up and walked past him. Then he opened a white-handled switchblade and plunged it into her. He pulled out the knife, folded it up again, and exited the Hub Bar, leaving her screaming, and returned to his post at the Sourdough. That's where the cops found Jack Ginsberg, the bloody knife in his pocket. Ginsberg's story wasn't quite what he pitched to the editor, since Ruby survived to testify against him in court.

Johnny wrote one word on the back of this snapshot: "Bombed." He made no effort to hide the degradation of alcoholism in Skid Row. Courtesy of John and Barbara Bacich.

Every night at the Sourdough, fifteen minutes before closing time, a particular crew of regulars would arrive. They wore the uniforms of the Minneapolis Police Department, and thanks to Johnny's regular liquid payoffs, the officers performed the nightly ritual changing of the guard. A quick jaunt by the city's finest through the crowded bar let everybody know they would be leaving shortly, without causing a fuss, or else feel the sting of a baton and perhaps a trip in the Black Maria. If they wanted to keep drinking, they would have to do it somewhere else.

If a gandy dancer made the decision to dry out and clean up, Johnny was ready to help. "If I liked him, I would put him in detox, but that never did work out half the time." Johnny told one sad story over and over again, and why it meant so much to him, I still don't know. The tragic figure was a handsome man from Iowa, who couldn't have been as young as Johnny said if he were a World War II veteran, but nonetheless the story goes like this:

He was one of my guys and he drank a lot. If you went to Holly-wood, got Bob Taylor, some of those Hollywood guys, none of them, none of them would hold a candle to this guy. He had beautiful dark hair, beautiful blue eyes, beautiful complexion, teeth that were made to order. I couldn't believe this guy. He was a young kid, about twenty. I said, "You know, I like you because you're a nice kid, nice-looking, clean-looking kid, God built you good. You come from a good family in Iowa. Why don't you sober up and go back to your family?" He didn't want to do it. But every once in a while, I'd have to take him to the hospital because he'd get so sick.

They told me at the veterans' hospital, because he was a veteran of World War II, they said, you know, he's going to die if he drinks any more. They had him in the hospital there one day I came and there were about eight nurses around him. What do you think they were doing?

Johnny waited for me to say, "I don't know."

They were observing how good-looking he was. The one nurse had told the rest.

I said, "Did anything happen?"

"Happen? Did you ever see anything so beautiful in your life?" My biggest mistake is I didn't take a picture of him.

He wanted to go home. He was in there, real sick. I said, "They want you to stay in, you're in bad shape, your liver is just about gone." He says, "Are you going to pick me up, or do I have to take the bus, because I want to get out of here."

"If you feel that way about it, fine, I'll pick you up." I picked him up, brought him back, put him in the little bed where he was. I said, "Here's something to eat, now please, don't drink." I was holding some money for him. He wanted the money. I said, "No, I know what you're going to do, you're going to drink." He said, "It's my money, Rex, and I mean it." "I'm not going to argue with you, I want to try to keep you from killing yourself. But here it is, remember what the doctor told you, you can't drink."

The guys tell you what's going on. He's down the block, in a bar, drinking like crazy, he's drunker than a skunk. Came back, next morning, nobody saw him. We looked in the cubicle. There he was, he was dead, twenty-one years old. What a shame, what a waste.

He had cast away any domestic life for this marriage to the bottle, oblivious to the women flitting around him. The beautiful kid from Iowa was buried at Fort Snelling at Johnny's expense.

In the memoir he dictated when he was in his early eighties, Johnny is usually restrained and philosophical. But on this subject he let loose: "I was so glad to get out of the liquor business. I was just fed up with it and I never knew why I ever got into it. It's a lousy, stinking business. People used to say, 'Well, John, if you don't get in the liquor business, somebody else will.' I said, 'Fine, let somebody else go in the liquor business then!' I've had my fill of it, and I don't want any more of it." As the destruction of the Gateway drew near, a convenient way to get out of the "lousy, stinking business" presented itself on a hot summer night. It was July 1961, and the Sourdough Bar went up in flames. But that was not the end.

⇒ 4 ⇐

THE FLOPHOUSE

It does not matter how small a cubicle is, the important
thing is that a man should be alone when he sleeps.
—George Orwell, *Down and Out in Paris and London*

The Victor Hotel, Johnny Rex, proprietor, had no grand entrance,
no doormen, no bellhops. The pillows were probably rock-hard,
and forget about any mints. The Victor was located at 21½ Second
Street South, in the same building as the Minnesota State Employment Service, which took up most of the ground floor and had a steady
stream of laborers coming in and out, that is, those who weren't finding jobs from the trucks pulling up to the "slave market" out front.
But the gandies who lived at the Victor weren't the ones lining up
for those jobs. They were the characters leaning up against the bricks
and giving a running commentary on the lousy, backbreaking, mis-
erably paying work that they were too old or lame or lazy or drunk to
do anymore. They might not have been paying attention at all, if one
of them had a bottle of rotgut. They would be standing obliviously
in a tight circle, passing the booze around.

A single door to the right of the employment service was labeled
"Victor Lodging House (no transients)." It opened to a steep flight
of stairs. Those stairs led to a second flight of stairs, and after that
ascent a small lobby appeared where a few gandies might be nursing a
bottle of Sweet Lucy, playing cards, or just sitting around. Or it might

be empty, with only the surly one-legged clerk Jim Larson behind the desk. If a person was new to the Victor, Larson might show the man to his room, which, like every hotel of its kind in the Gateway, had corridor after corridor of closely spaced doors, about twenty on a floor. The walls of each room were made of plywood and tin, with nails to hang clothes and, instead of a ceiling, chicken wire with a bare bulb hanging through. Welcome to your cage.

If a man didn't like the Victor, he didn't even have to leave the block to find other lodging. There was the Pioneer on the corner of Nicollet and Second, home to a cheerful lobby painted in bright red and yellow, and shabby bay windows that gave it a sense of faded grandeur. Nearby were the Foster, the Senate, the Beacon, the Acme, and some seventy other lodging houses crammed into eighteen square blocks, available for about fifty measly cents a night, cheaper by the week, even less by the month. Tenants who paid in advance didn't have to worry about losing their housing if they got jackrolled, which happened all the time.

Johnny Rex may have owned two flophouses, maybe four. But the Victor is the only one he really remembered. It was one of the great cage hotels, a form of Skid Row lodging that has nearly disappeared in twenty-first-century America, but one that was familiar to the down-and-out for generations. No building was ever designed as a cage hotel, but it was easy enough to adapt the upper floors of an old store or warehouse. Minneapolis's first cage hotel appeared in 1892, as a place to sleep for the lumberjacks, construction workers, and other seasonal laborers flooding into the booming city of the Northwest. The former head of the Union City Mission, Rev. William E. Paul, wrote that the design was actually borrowed from "floating hotels"—converted ferries docked in Cleveland and other

The Victor Hotel occupied the top two floors of this old commercial building at 21–21½ Second Street South. The Minnesota State Employment Service on the ground floor placed those willing to work in general labor jobs. Photograph by Norton & Peel. Courtesy of the Minnesota Historical Society.

5-9 C&D 08-03-60
R.G. PALEN

Two steep flights of stairs led to the lobbies of the flophouses.
This was the view of the stairway to the Pioneer Hotel, at Second
and Nicollet. Courtesy of the City of Minneapolis.

Great Lakes ports that could house two hundred guests. They were
originally built for boat crews, but then opened up to anybody who
could pay. Somebody figured out a "cubicle" or cage hotel could be
built on dry land as well, so they started converting buildings in cities
across the country. By 1895 the number of cage hotels had grown to
fifty in Minneapolis alone. These places might have seemed spartan
to most people, but for men used to sleeping in rail cars, labor camps,
and sawmills, they felt just like home.

In cities across the nation, similar low-rent lodging districts emerged

The lobby and dayroom of the Pioneer Hotel offered a space for card playing, smoking, or just a place to let your belly hang out. A sign on the wall announces the new room rates: seventy-five cents a night. Courtesy of the City of Minneapolis.

to serve a seasonal labor force. Those jobs had mostly vanished by the mid-twentieth century, and "skid road," a logging term from the Pacific Northwest that gave its name to a low-rent quarter of Seattle, morphed into Skid Row. The cheap lodging districts now served a more permanent population of laborers too old or feeble or injured for hard labor. They had "hit the skids" and now slept in human cubbyholes in the oldest sections of North America's industrial cities. It wasn't unusual in those days to label people who lived in hotels

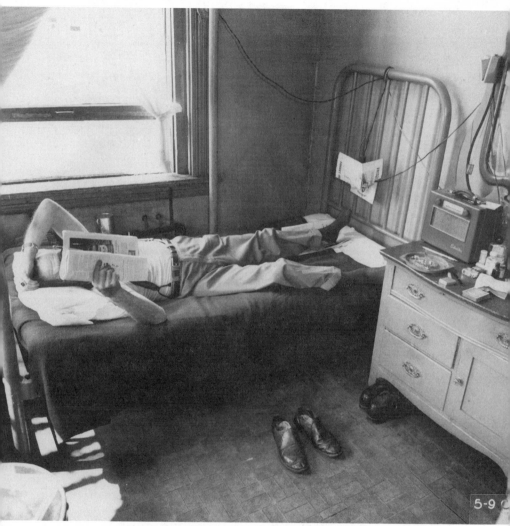

5-9

The cubicles had room for a bed, a dresser, and not much else, but they offered privacy. The chicken wire ceilings prevented thieves from entering the spaces from above. This resident of the Pioneer Hotel hid behind his magazine when the photographer hired by the city stopped by. Courtesy of the City of Minneapolis.

as homeless. Traditional families—husband, wife, and children—stood atop the pantheon in 1950s America. Living alone was supposed to be a temporary state, and if it went on for long, something must be wrong with you. Yet an estimated eighteen thousand men (and six hundred women) called New York City's Bowery home in 1952. A 1963 survey in Chicago found more than seventy-five hundred people living in cage hotels. They had good reasons to live in those places. A cheap meal, a used suit, a free haircut, a ten-cent beer, a park bench, the reading room of the library, all were within walking distance. But this kind of community, with many uses in one place, conflicted with recent zoning laws, a new tool in early twentieth-century planning. Zoning separated and segregated the many functions of a city that sought to impose some permanent lines and rules on the ever-evolving urban landscape. Associating hotels with a more transient population, planners classified these places as public nuisances in the mid-twentieth century. They were blamed for shiftlessness and crime, and hotels that catered to single women who worked downtown were accused of fostering sexual immorality and undermining the family.

As early as the 1890s, Minneapolis began to worry about Bridge Square, the downtown neighborhood named for the first bridge built over the Mississippi River. It was the city's oldest quarter, site of the original city hall, and close to its two train stations. Any newcomer looking for a place to stay near the Great Northern or Milwaukee Depots would find dozens to choose from, though all of them would convey the impression of a city that had fallen on some hard times. In 1918 the city outlawed the opening of any new cage hotels, but it did nothing about the many that were already in business. The massive Nicollet Hotel on Washington Avenue was built in 1924 to bring a better class of accommodations to the area, and for years it loomed over the pavilion in Gateway Park. Unlike other hotels in the area, the Nicollet retained its cachet well into the 1950s. That was about all it did. "The Nicollet Hotel, the city's finest, is surrounded by dumps," noted Lait and Mortimer, the traveling scandal-sniffing newspaper columnists who wrote *U.S.A. Confidential.* "One of the most degrading places we have ever seen is a hell-hole called the Nicollet Inn, across the street from the swank hotel." What was so awful about the Nicollet Inn, 225 Nicollet, they left to the imagination.

I don't know whether Lait and Mortimer made it around the corner, but they probably would have had little good to say about the Victor Hotel. In a structure built with a more grandiose mercantile purpose, the Victor still looked fancy from the outside. It stood three stories high, crowned with a studded cornice in the Italianate commercial style popular in the nineteenth century. Over the years, the ground-floor storefront had lost its original character, but the second and third stories retained their rows of tall, double-hung windows with elegant hoods—peaked on the second floor, rounded on the third. It might have been a nice place, once, before the neighborhood went to seed and the upper floors of all the buildings had been turned into colonies of the lost, the soused, and the exiled.

In Skid Row Minneapolis, people lived in their cages for years, and some for decades. Their home was so small, maybe thirty-six square feet, that it must have felt as cozy as a womb. A graduate student wandering through the Gateway in the late 1950s found two guys who had lived in their cubicles since 1933. One resident described the accommodations as a partition of boards and chicken wire, lit with a dim twenty-watt bulb, dirty, and offering a consistent chance that the occupant would get "lousy." The other guests, whose heads could be only a few inches from yours, snoring on the other side of the thin plywood, might be less than neighborly. Whatever you had in your possession, someone wanted it more than you did and was willing to do whatever it took to separate it from you. One gandy had a pair of shoes that apparently struck someone else's fancy. One night, as he snoozed in his cage, someone dropped a string with a hook through the chicken wire, "caught" the shoes, and reeled them in. Yet the men who lived there did their best to make their cubicles their own. They decorated what little wall space they had with pin-ups, no frames needed. These were the only reminders of women in an all-male colony, and it was pornography that now looks charmingly quaint. The women's legs are tastefully folded, their breasts shaped in the missile-nose-cone fashion of the atomic age, their smiling pretty faces reminding these worn-out men of their youth.

A gandy dancer sits for his portrait in the Victor Hotel, his window overlooking Second Street South. Johnny said he did not allow transients, meaning every resident paid by the month. Courtesy of John and Barbara Bacich.

As for the occupants' earthly possessions, the shoes were tucked neatly under the bed. Clothes were hung on hangers, and the hangers on nails. They might have a small dresser, covered with newspaper, and a chair. Back in 1958, Samuel Wallace paid sixty cents for a four-by-six-foot room. He rested his head on a "small, unbelievably hard pillow." He opened the small cabinet at the head of the steel bed and found a washbowl, a paper bag, a beer opener, matches, religious tracts, a hand towel, an ashtray, and a busted mirror. Long-term tenants tended to accumulate more possessions, just like anyone else who stays in one place, although what they collected wasn't always conventional. Johnny Rex remembered one guy who had maybe a

The cubicles were so small that your guest sat side by side with you on your bed. Johnny could not remember the names of these guys. Courtesy of John and Barbara Bacich.

hundred watches that weren't worth three bucks put together. Graduate student Keith Lovald cataloged the more exotic possessions with forensic precision. "A new tire, a bicycle frame, a large wooden box filled with miscellaneous hardware, piles of old newspapers and magazines, a roll of copper tubing, a deer's head, a toilet seat and an automobile steering wheel." The hoarders kept more than junk. A man by the name of Amen Balkin lived in a flop called the Oslo Hotel, and he kept the proceeds from his odd jobs in a gunnysack, because the Depression erased any confidence he had in banks. For some reason, the management of the Oslo Hotel threw Balkin out in 1955, so he hauled his sack to the police station for safekeeping. The officers sent him to a bank, where it took eight people to count out his nest egg: $5,754. The number was probably higher before the police compensated themselves for their trouble.

In a flophouse cubicle, an occupant might be able to entertain one visitor who was sitting on a chair. Otherwise, they were sitting side by side on the bed, an intimate arrangement but certainly convenient for sharing a bottle. One time Johnny shot a picture of two weathered fellows with big smiles sitting next to each other on a bed that seems to have no sheet. He did not remember their names. There's a table crowded with coffee cups, glasses, and other junk and a window, a luxury for the end units, looking out on the street. Larger gatherings were reserved for the common room, the lobby, or the alleys. Johnny once packed sixty-seven gandies in the Victor, so many men they were doubled up in some of the cages, or sacked out on the couches he had gotten from the Salvation Army and parked in the lobby. Not everybody had to pay, Johnny pointed out. He also emphatically discouraged certain potential guests. There was a girls high school basketball team from out of town that wrote a letter to ask for eight rooms at the Victor during a tournament. Johnny advised them to look elsewhere, and he chuckled about the idea of these innocent young ladies sharing the floor with his hard-bitten gandies, as if they have might have cooked and eaten the girls on the spot.

For conventional hotel guests, the Victor and its fellow flophouses were not the most hospitable of places. In November 1957, a visitor to Minneapolis from Niarada, Montana, named Theodore Griddle had the misfortune to check into the Victor. Griddle ended up trading his cage at the Victor for a bed at the General Hospital. Perhaps seeing an easy mark on a Saturday night, six men pummeled Griddle and relieved him of twenty dollars in traveler's checks—not a fortune, but if they somehow managed to cash them, worth two hundred glasses of beer at the nearby Sourdough. I found that story in a yellowing clipping in the basement archive of the *Star Tribune*, and it was apparently the only mention of the Victor Hotel in the history of the newspaper. Nothing else in the history of the place, none of the antics or talents or remarkable tales of the men who spent a good part of their lives there, apparently piqued other reporters' interest enough to write a story about it.

Johnny had no memory of the robbery of Mr. Griddle, or why he spent a night in the Victor. But he did know how rough his place could be. One of his more occasional guests was a man of large stature—six foot nine inches, 240 pounds, in Johnny's estimation. He was a farmer who came to the big city to seek pleasures unavailable outstate. After a morning bender, the farmer thumped up the stairs toward a confrontation with the proprietor, a foot shorter than he was. "He was drunker than a skunk," Johnny recalled, and the latest contender for the challenge of decking the proprietor:

He said, "Rex, I'm going to knock you off your feet."

"Go lay down in your cage and go to sleep," I said.

So he grabbed me on the shoulders and I learned where you go underneath, put your arms around and spread his arms and kick them to the side, and then you hit him. And I hit him with a right and he went down. He shook his head, got up again, and said:

"Well, damn you."

Johnny hit him again, with a left. The giant farmer toppled to the floor. He didn't get up.

I said to the guys, "Pick him up and take him to his flop." So they took him into his cage there and locked it up so he couldn't get out.

He sobered up about six hours later. He woke up around five o'clock and he came out and came into my office:

"Rex, do you know what happened to me?"

"No."

"I fell down those damned steps. I almost killed myself."

The gandies laughed like crazy.

Johnny's memoir, dictated in 2002 and 2003, reads in parts like a catalog of fisticuffs, although it also states that he hated fighting. Still, the old tank commander ran his flophouse like a military base, and he was proud of it. The gandies would muster every Saturday for inspection, and Johnny would look over the floors and the rooms and the toilets. Whoever had the cleanest got a free gallon of wine. But Johnny saw to it that the other ones got something for their effort. Indeed, wine flowed freely at the Victor—Lovald, the sociology student, noted that the Victor stood apart from the other flops in its tolerance of tippling in the lobby.

"As a matter of fact," Lovald wrote, "the residents are encouraged to drink. The operator of the Victor retains the old Hobohemian practice of taking rent out of monthly checks. With the remainder, the men are issued meal tickets and to make the arrangement more interesting, he brings in an occasional case of wine from his nearby liquor store. Gandy dancers are apt to prefer this system."

I read that passage to Johnny as he sat in his living room, fifty years later, and asked whether Lovald's observation was accurate. He grunted and made a skeptical face, but he didn't exactly deny it. In Johnny's world, the liquor was the fuel that kept Skid Row going, and it was his job to give these men what they wanted, when they wanted it.

Not every hotel was so outwardly supportive of its tippling tenants. A scene captured by one of the eavesdropping graduate students makes you wonder who was worse, the staggering obnoxious resident or the congenitally nasty flophouse manager:

A drunk, one of the hotel residents, entered the lobby. He addressed the manager of the hotel.

"Hello there, Mr. Mason."

"Go on, get away from me. I ain't got no god damn use for drunks. You know that, so get away from me or I'll throw you out."

"Oh now Charlie . . ."

"You heard me. Get away. All my trouble comes from drunks and I ain't got no use for 'em. Get away."

Charlie came out from behind the desk and the drunk headed for his room.

One wonders why Mr. Mason, if he had such an aversion to people who drank heavily, would choose to work as the manager of a hotel in the ocean of booze known as Skid Row. If the sociologists ever pursued this question, it has been lost to history. But Mason did offer this bit of wisdom: "God damn drunken bastards. The other guys bitch to me about all the trouble they have from drunks. Well, I been on the avenue over eleven years now and I guess everybody knows I don't put up with drunks."

Some of the flophouses featured signs that said, "Money refunded if drunk." The clerks were the enforcers, and behind the desk they kept a blunt instrument handy in case anybody put up a fuss. In another unconventional research exercise, a graduate student pretended to be blotto and tried to check into one of the flophouses. The clerk took out a hammer, started swinging it around, and chased him out. They weren't all bluster, either. On a February night in 1957, a man was discovered staggering, bloodied and dazed, in the streets. The cops found a second man, somewhere else in the Lower Loop, suffering similar damage. Their names were James Ericksen and Henry Larsen, and they told the same story. Ericksen, resident of the Pioneer Hotel, was hosting his friend Larsen, who was visiting from the Beacon Hotel. The two were having a drink when the night manager, Harold Bradley, confronted their private wine-tasting session with apparent displeasure. The situation became so inflamed that Bradley smashed each of them on the head with a blackjack. All three were carted off to jail: Bradley to face an assault charge, Larsen on a charge of intoxication, and Ericksen just to make sure he stayed around long enough to grant an interview to the cops.

Two months after that fracas, the clerk at the Elmo Hotel a block away was apparently an accomplice to debauchery. It was 2:15 in the morning when somebody complained about a disturbance inside the Elmo. Police found six men and five women. Only seven of them were wearing clothes (the nude ones were equally divided between men and women). One of them, a visitor from Duluth, had the unfortunate name of Mr. Hornyak. The clerk, Roland A. Gerth, was among the men—whether he was in the buff was not noted in the story. He was busted for failing to register the guests' real names, apparently violating another city rule designed to maintain decency among the indecent.

In the cage hotels, the rules were posted on the walls in large letters. Sometimes they exuded customer service: "To our guests, we provide clean comfortable rooms and want you to feel at home here. The manager will personally welcome any complaints." Other policies were less friendly: "No cash refund. No credit." One can't help but feel a little sorry for the men working behind the desks. It must have been a dreadful job. There was always the chance they would get robbed, or worse. Two night clerks at the A&C Hotel were slugged when they wouldn't let two drunk guys get a room at 3:15 a.m. one winter night in 1953. From Johnny's perspective, though, the clerks were the ones mistreating him. For a long time, one of his residents, Jim Larson, staffed the front desk of the Victor Hotel. Johnny let him live in one of the cubicles rent-free for doing this job. Larson had an artificial leg and liked to hurt people. He was, in Johnny's recollection, a "sadist" (Johnny pronounced it like "saddest"). According to Johnny, Larson also had a secret agreement with the owner of the building, "Dago Mike," to steal benefit checks from the other gandies, forge their signatures, and cash them. Somehow they got away with this scheme for a long time, and Johnny didn't find out about it until long after he had fired Larson for some other infraction. The revelation came when the three men were sitting down together in Dago Mike's bar on Broadway Street. Larson and Dago Mike found it all quite funny as they told Johnny how they ripped him off, undetected, for so long. Johnny now understands why the authorities were constantly accusing him of tampering with his gandies' checks. He was

Signs behind the front desk at the Pioneer Hotel lay out the rules in block letters. Clerks had to maintain order amid the sometimes drunken antics of their guests. Courtesy of the City of Minneapolis.

still sore about it when we met. In Johnny's world, everyone was constantly stealing, scamming, hustling—no one could be trusted. While he firmly believed everyone on Skid Row was a thief, he somehow took it personally when he saw it happen in his own business.

It's no wonder some of the city's most unsavory characters found business opportunities on Skid Row. One door down from Rex Liquors was the A&C Hotel, 203 Nicollet, whose proprietor was a large fellow with a taste for cigars named Morris "Big Mose" Barnett. Johnny knew enough about him to keep his distance. Big Mose at one time was the most feared gangster in Minneapolis. Back in the 1920s, Big Mose tipped the scales at 240 pounds, not counting the iron in his pocket. He regularly threw that weight around to enforce the mob's control over the city's laundry businesses, a lucrative monopoly that complemented his gambling and bootlegging enterprises. In the summer of 1927 a Minneapolis shopkeeper named Sam Shapiro refused to shut down his dry cleaning plant, which competed with the mob-controlled cleaners. The dispute escalated, and on August 20, 1927, Big Mose and his henchmen invaded Shapiro's store on Franklin Avenue. They sprayed sulfuric acid on the clothes dropped off by Shapiro's customers, and then smashed the dry cleaner in the head with the butt of a pistol. That was one act of thuggery too many. A corruption investigation later uncovered Big Mose's malfeasances, which included bribing the police chief. He went on the run for several years, but the heat caught up with him; he surrendered and served four years in prison. A generation passed. Big Mose had lost considerable poundage, not to mention influence, and reinvented himself as a flophouse manager.

On a cold day in 1953, a fire at the A&C Hotel cut short a party for nine guests and sent them wobbling into the street. The cops hauled them to jail. Big Mose went to court and took the side of his guests, now defendants.

"These men, your honor, are men of principle," the big old reformed gangster told the judge, as if he recognized the type. "They work on the railroad, have money and pay their bills.

"They were doing a little social drinking last night in their rooms

William Bridges, Gust Tarsuk, and Clifford Christjohn play cards in the day room at the Pioneer Hotel. Johnny remembered that the hotel's proprietor, Charlie Arnold, had a mansion in Southern California. Photograph by Larry Schreiber, *Minneapolis Star Tribune*. Courtesy of the Minnesota Historical Society.

The dayroom at the Acme Hotel, 223½ Marquette Avenue South, in February 1961. As his tenants played cards or looked on, the Acme's owner, Morris "Big Mose" Barnett stood at the right, cigar in hand. Barnett had been a notorious gangster who served time in prison and found a new profession running flophouses. Courtesy of the City of Minneapolis.

and bothering no one. It was not their fault they had to go into the street."

The judge accepted the love-fest explanation and called Big Mose's character reference "highly commendable." The judge meted out ten-dollar fines for each guy, but said they did not have to pay and sent them on their way. Big Mose approached the bench, and the onetime "king of the underworld" shook hands with the judge. It turns out judges were some of the people who paid visits to Big Mose in 1965 when he was dying in his room at the Home At Last rooming house. He owned that one, too, and Home At Last's location at 1500 Stevens Avenue was safely out of the way of the Gateway renewal bulldozers. Big Mose Barnett's time on Skid Row, strangely, had burnished his reputation.

To those who studied the Gateway, particularly from the perspective of wanting to remove it—and everyone who lived in it—from the face of the earth forever, the place was seemingly in danger of bursting into flames at any moment. Decrepit old buildings constructed before 1880 probably had ancient wiring, piles of flammable junk, and plenty of lit cigarettes constantly falling from the lips and hands of passed-out geezers. The flophouses "are filled with the old and feeble, the slow moving, the hard-of-hearing, and the drunks," making them the worst kind of people to evacuate from a fast-moving fire, wrote Wallace, the Skid Row chronicler. The inside pages of the newspapers featured short items about flophouse residents setting their mattresses on fire. The danger was so obvious that the city had an ordinance that prohibited smoking in bed in a hotel, but that didn't stop the occasional flare-up. In March 1956, Alvin Opsal lived at the Beaufort Hotel, 112 Third Street South, and even as his health failed, he refused to go into a hospital. He also refused to give up smoking. One morning his cigarette started a blaze, and the smoke overcame him. Firefighters finally carried him out of the Beaufort, and a newspaper photographer captured the moment, with Opsal's mouth open and his eyes skyward. He died a couple of days later, only sixty years old. In 1959 Leonard D. Gladstone got sixty days in jail after accidentally igniting his bed at the Foster Hotel, a few doors down from the Victor. It was a harsh punishment for immolating one's own bedding, but then again, it was the seventh time in eight years Gladstone had torched his mattress.

By the 1950s, the city wasn't leaving the safety of these places up to chance. In 1955 one of my predecessors at the newspaper, editorial page staffer Jay Edgerton, accompanied a health inspector on his rounds of the Gateway flophouses. Edgerton paints a portrait of filth and degradation, which stayed above the realm of abject debasement

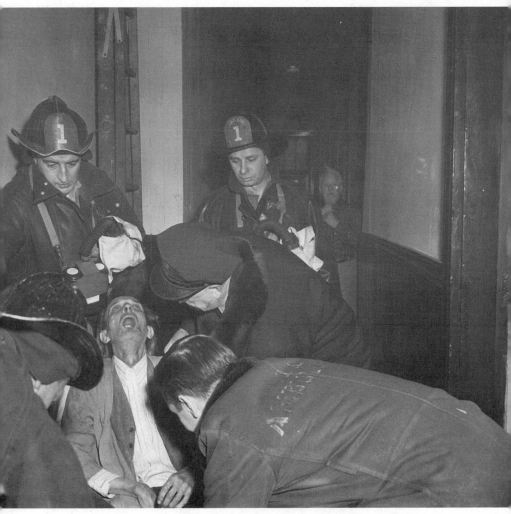

Alvin Opsal, who lived at the Beaufort Hotel, 112 Third Street
South, refused to give up smoking, and it cost him his life. In
March 1956, overcome by smoke after he accidentally set his
room on fire, Opsal was carried out by Minneapolis firefighters.
He died in the hospital. Photograph by the *Minneapolis Star
Tribune*. Courtesy of the Minnesota Historical Society.

The toilets at the Pioneer Hotel did not offer much privacy. University of Minnesota researchers detected a severe plumbing shortage in Skid Row, where the ratio of residents to toilets was 10 to 1. Courtesy of the City of Minneapolis.

only through the tireless efforts of the Minneapolis Department of Health's inspectors, in this case, Mr. Merwin B. Oyen. Edgerton does not name the establishments he and Oyen visited, but he does offer some vivid imagery on his ride-along with the regulator of Skid Row's standard of living. Oyen ordered one fellow to clean up a stinking toilet, and notes another spot on a wall stained brown from repeated spittings of tobacco juice. "By any normal standards," Edgerton writes, "the sights and smells of skid row are enough to turn the visitor's stomach."

For so many visitors to Skid Row, it was all about the smell. "Here again the odor of insecticide hangs heavy in the air. Added to it is the musty smell of an old building and the mingled stenches of perspiration, dirty clothes, tobacco, liquor and unwashed socks." One hundred fifty men might share one commode, and no plumbing can handle that kind of use without complaint. A later historian, Joseph Hart, described it this way: "The odor of these overused toilets mingled in the open-ceilinged cages with cigarette smoke, the aroma of surreptitious hot-plate stews, and the rank musk of aged men unused to bathing." Lovald's nose detected the cuisine from illegal hot plates reheating beans and cans of soup, whose odor "permeates the already overburdened atmosphere in several of the hotels and lodging houses." One time a flophouse denizen offered to share a can of beans and a cup of coffee with the visiting university student. Lovald declined, but found the act of generosity worth noting in his monograph. At times, though, he found the smell of the hotels so overpowering that he had to break off his interview to bolt down the stairs and out into the street to keep from losing his lunch.

After they lived in that environment for years, the olfactory capacity of the residents must have been severely impaired. One day, a persistent foul odor in the Victor Hotel started to bother Johnny Rex, and the ensuing Saturday cleaning day could not banish it. He told his gandies to figure out what it was. They could not smell the odor, though, so he helped them trace it to the room of a fellow they had not seen for a while. It turns out the occupant had been dead for sixteen days. At this point in his story, Johnny informed me that the cops hated to handle people in this condition, because corpses tend to bloat, especially in the heat, and when picked up, they can explode, with loathsome consequences for anyone nearby. Nowadays, John observed, they just put them in a bag and zip them up, thereby containing any rupture that occurs in transit. He was a man who believed in American progress.

The death of a tenant at the Victor was an event that once prompted a visit from Big Mose Barnett. Guests would sometimes migrate from the old gangster's establishments, the A&C or the Acme, and move into Johnny's flophouse, and Big Mose liked to keep tabs on them. Johnny remembered one uncomfortable encounter with Big Mose after a guest expired at the Victor.

"Did you search him?" Big Mose asked. "Did you see if he had any money?"

"No," Johnny said.

"You're crazy! Christ, they have money sewed into their coats. You didn't check them? Police go through them pretty good."

For Johnny, it wasn't worth it. He didn't want anything to do with a corpse. If the stiff was a veteran, and many of them were, Johnny would pay for his burial at the National Cemetery at Fort Snelling. If the deceased persons weren't veterans, well, who knows? They wouldn't mind being buried in a potter's field. Johnny was content to let them take their money with them.

By the Gateway's final days, the cage hotel as a form of housing was already on its way out. Dozens were swept away by urban renewal, not only in Minneapolis but all over the country, especially along West Madison Street in Chicago, where thousands of men once snored their nights away under bare bulbs and chicken wire. At least one Chicago cage hotel was still in business in 2012—the Ewing Annex Hotel on South Clark Street, although you wouldn't know it by that name: the sign, in the same building that is home to Royal Pawn and Coco's Deep Fried Lobster, only says "Hotel" and below it "Men Only." I spotted that place while wandering south of the Loop and wondered why a hotel advertised itself by its gender limitations.

By 2000 only about eight flophouses—most of them cage joints— were left on America's most famous Skid Row, the Bowery. A cage cost a bargain $4.50 a night. While New York spared the Bowery from large-scale demolition, Skid Row couldn't resist the inexorable force of gentrification sweeping across the island of Manhattan. One of those establishments, the old Prince Hotel, was renamed Bowery House and converted into more comfortable but still cramped accommodations catering to German, Swedish, and French tourists for a hundred bucks a night. The second floor, however, remained in the service of its traditional tenants, for whom a hundred bucks would actually pay for two weeks' residency.

When I visited the old flophouse in 2012, it was as if I had walked out of Soho and back in time to old New York. The first thing I noticed was the elegant tiled floor, which consisted of concentric hexagons in white and brown. That was the extent of the Bowery House's elegance, however. The heavy bars of the clerk's cage were to my left, and the sentry post appeared to be unmanned. I could see worn wooden cubbyholes, and inside them were blocks of wood attached to keys, like the kind restaurants use to keep people from walking away with their restroom keys. I met a man there who said his name was Ray Martinez. He was short and round, maybe in his late fifties or early sixties, with limp gray hair poking out from under his cap. Twenty years ago, he had a fight with his girlfriend and moved out of their apartment. He found a cubicle at 220 Bowery, and he had lived there ever since. It was doubtful he would be there for twenty more, though. There were only nine people left in a hotel that once had two hundred cages. Wait, Ray corrected himself, eight people. One guy was in the hospital.

We walked down narrow corridors flanked by doors leading to what were human closets, but most were now empty, the metal beds standing on their ends. We passed a grim-looking bathroom and turned left. The coveted corner unit, with a luxurious two windows, was Ray's home. I would estimate it was six feet by six feet, but only a small patch of floor space was visible because it was taken up by a bed, a dresser, a refrigerator, and a television. The ceiling consisted of plastic lattice, the kind you get at hardware stores to grow vines on. I asked if I could take a picture. Ray said no, he wanted to tidy up first.

I asked Ray if the place got noisy. He told me TVs had to be off by 11 p.m., but people could keep watching if they wore head-phones. We walked back to the lobby. I had one last question—why was there a safe in the middle of the floor? "Used to be a lot of money in there," he said. "Not anymore." I detected a wistful note in his voice.

Fifty years earlier and fifteen hundred miles west, when the federal money finally came and the wrecking machines arrived in Skid Row to excise the "cancer" in Minneapolis's urban landscape, the first stop was the Vendome Hotel on Fourth Street South. It seemed fitting to knock down a flophouse first, since no other Skid Row institution seemed more problematic to those in charge of the city's future. Everybody had probably paid a visit to one of the rowdy bars or picked up a bottle of booze or maybe even shopped at one of the non-bum-oriented stores in the Lower Loop. But to live there, to say it was your home, that was truly a marker that you had hit bottom. So one by one the hotels emptied out at the city's order: the Milner, the Anchor, the Pioneer, the Denver, the Washington, the Senate, the Beaufort, and every other cage hotel and fleabag and mission flop. For a few years, much of the neighborhood stood vacant. In 1960 and 1961, the city sent photographers into each of those buildings to document everything—from the basements to the broom closets and the electrical panels and the narrow staircases with their heavily varnished newel posts. You can catch glimpses of the vanished lives there: a hanger left on a hook, a balled-up pair of pants on a chair, a calendar on a wall that counted down the days to oblivion. In the trashed lobby of the old A&C Hotel, once run by Big Mose Barnett up above Johnny's liquor store, a cheerful sign over a doorway beckons to no one: "To our guests and gandy friends." Another sign hangs at a slant, still attached by only one tack: "Luggage will not be held

A hallway of empty rooms is still mostly intact in the abandoned A&C Hotel, 203 Nicollet Avenue, in December 1960. The city outlawed new cubicle hotels in 1918, but this minimalist housing persisted well into the post–World War II era. Courtesy of the City of Minneapolis.

10-2&3
12-7-60

over 30 days." The cubbyholes for mail are all empty, there's rubbish on the floor, and someone has left an empty pint bottle on the old clerk's desk, one last dead soldier.

Fairly soon, the last cage hotel anywhere in the nation will be converted into an artist's loft or a yoga studio or maybe just a parking lot. To modern eyes, these rooms may resemble a prison, but from what I could see these cages were not places of confinement. They were a refuge, the lowest common denominator of privacy but private nonetheless, a place for a man to shut his flimsy door against the chaos of the world, lie back on his pillow, and look up into a chicken wire sky. For all the noise and the stench and the filth and the decrepitude, he could close his eyes and know he was home.

$$\equiv 5 \equiv$$

MISSIONS

"If you don't start behaving like a Christian, I'll throw
you out. In Jesus' name, the Lord be praised."
—Skid Row mission preacher admonishing
a drunk in the pews

Johnny Rex's rambler on Harriet Avenue South in Minneapolis sat
on a double lot with a big blooming garden that sprawled over the
backyard. Every Sunday, the bells would toll from the Church of the
Annunciation at the end of his block, and if he was feeling particularly Catholic that day, he could take his place in the pews in about
forty-five seconds. The first time I walked up to his door, I noticed
the sign to the left, propped in a window. It had three lines written
in large, black, stenciled lettering:

No guns. No dogs. No missionaries.

Like many people, Johnny Rex had a complicated relationship
with religion, and I can understand that, considering that he was, to
the Bible thumpers of the Gateway, the Devil incarnate. From the
missionaries' point of view, he was the one who peddled booze to
drunks, keeping them chained to a life of sloth and venality through
a vertically integrated alcoholic enterprise. In Johnny's view, the
preachers were as mercenary as anybody else in that part of town, if

not more so. They made good money, he would say. He paid as little attention to them as possible. Even if Johnny could ignore the other evangelists, and their tinny gospel hymns blaring from speakers out into the street, he always had to walk past the Harvest Field Mission. It was one of the smaller evangelistic establishments, and it occupied a storefront at 19 Second Street South. Anyone traveling between Rex Liquors and the Victor Hotel, and there were many, passed by the little church and its door with the cheerful painted words, "Welcome In." The mission was strategically located next to Party Alley, the principal gathering place for the spontaneous bottle gangs, where many a beverage purchased at Rex Liquors was consumed. Only a masonry wall separated the devotional from the debauched. No one could really measure the distance between the men passing the bottle and those seated inside, taking an "ear beating" from a man who was once down and out, just like them, and now worked full-time to show them the light. On a cold winter night, though, the Harvest Field Mission welcomed desperate men who would otherwise freeze to death. In those circumstances, sleeping on the floor or two chairs pushed together felt like deliverance.

The missions were set up to save the gandy dancers from themselves, yet the Gateway really wasn't the Gateway without them. Skid Row as a community depended on the gandies, thrived on them, provided them sustenance for their stomachs and their spirits, and gave meaning to those who would steer Skid Rowers onto a more wholesome path. "The men on Skid Row seem to sense that perhaps the missions need them more than they need the missions," sociologist Sam Wallace observed. For outcasts, the men of Skid Row sure had plenty of people who wanted to get to know them better.

In the early part of the twentieth century, the missions' precursors were city-run lodging houses, the homeless shelters of their day. These were set up to discourage vagrancy and begging, but quickly gained the same notoriety these places always do. In 1911 Minneapolis opened its lodging house in an old jail, and not surprisingly, the facility never really caught on. The lodging house shut down within a decade. Once it closed, the missions moved in to provide emergency shelter. Where the institutions of City Beautiful

Shown here shortly after its relocation, the Harvest Field Mission, 19 Second Street South, offered a refuge between the Victor Hotel and Rex Liquors. A sociologist observed that missions needed Skid Row's lost souls more than the men actually needed the missions. Courtesy of the City of Minneapolis.

had failed, the institutions of the City on a Hill were determined to succeed. The Salvation Army's Harbor Light, House of Charity, Minneapolis Revival Mission, Gateway Gospel Mission, and all the others had a simple formula: drunk = evil, sober = good. No fewer than nine rescue missions were operating in 1958, cheek by jowl with the venues of earthly degradation.

By feeding the homeless and offering them shelter, sometimes only a spot on the floor, the missions no doubt saved many lives. Their record of saving souls is thinner. University researchers concluded that most of those attending the mandatory services that preceded free meals contributed their bodies, not their minds. The prerecorded hymns played through the speakers signaled the start of services. The men shuffled in, took their seats at the back, and someone tapped out some devotional music on an old piano. Then the sermon began. The university students wrote down some of the highlights they heard.

"My heart, listen, you won't believe it, my heart is breaking because of my own lethargy, it is burning and breaking because of my own lethargy, sinner, friend, where are you going tonight when God's holy word comes to fulfillment? Where are you hiding?"

"When you go out this door tonight, you'll go either as (a) a Christian, or (b) a reprobate . . . I remember my father telling me that back as a kid. Would you rather love your Christian brethern . . . er, that is your brethern, or would you rather be in a tavern and be with that kind of people, leading the life of sin of skid row, damning your soul to Hell?"

If the preacher went on too long, the congregation would scrape their feet and cough and talk until he got the message and shut up. Yet if you were moved by the sermon, instead of putting up with it, if it truly seized something in your chest and lifted you out of your chair and you were standing, ready to give yourself up to Jesus, then you did not have to wait for your reward in heaven. The missions typically set aside a number of beds for the evening's converts so they wouldn't have to sleep on the hard floor. On most nights, though, no one ever warmed those sheets. Committing to the mission meant attending all services, taking showers every day, getting your clothing fumigated, and offering public testimonies of your return to grace. It

A man eats in a Skid Row mission in Minneapolis, 1959. Jerome Liebling wrote: "I photographed in the flophouses, bars, and streets of the Gateway for several years; the photographs reflect the struggle that so many faced in their attempts to hold on and make their way." Photograph courtesy of the Minnesota Historical Society. Copyright Jerome Liebling Photography.

was a hard pill to swallow, and you couldn't wash it down with muscatel. Converts were few. The mission workers had to learn to accept failure, night after night, because they probably knew that anyone who embraced the mission life was automatically considered, among the professional drinkers outside, a traitor. In the pecking order of Skid Row, no one was lower than the "mission stiff." The feeling was mutual. Like prisoner trustees in jail, the mission stiffs felt entitled to boss around the guys who wandered in, looking for some help. A mission worker in the late 1950s gave his view of why men ended up in Skid Row: "The major reason is that they were all spoiled as children, they could have what they wanted as children. And they are still spoiled today."

Still, a cup of coffee and a couple of stale pieces of bread smeared with margarine were reason enough for untold numbers of Skid Rowers to endure an hour of homilies and hymns, with all the standing and sitting and bowing of heads. It's worth noting here that these men did not have the healthiest diet already. The typical Gateway restaurant was a "slop joint." To our great fortune, Samuel Wallace preserved one slop joint's menu and published it in his book. It's handwritten on a piece of paper with the logo of Grain Belt Premium beer at the bottom, accompanied by the slogan "The perfect companion for fine food . . ." So what was this fine food? Bean soup was the soupe du jour. Just underneath it was fried walleyed pike, for sixty cents. Canned sardines with a side of potato salad was a mere fifty cents. A half dollar could also buy you the unique combination of lamb stew and spaghetti. Big spenders could get the beef tenderloin for a buck fifty. Chili or hot tamales were only twenty-five cents. Restaurants also served something called "coffee-ans," as in, coffee and a stale Danish, a kind of handout for anyone who had a dime for the coffee. This cuisine may sound unappetizing, but it was the comfort food of the down-and-out. One former Gateway resident even showed up at the city relocation office, months after he had been moved out of the demolition zone, saying he wanted to move back, because "nowhere could he find roast pork and applesauce like he could get on the 'Avenue.'"

A customer sits at the counter of Ray's Lunch, a typical Skid Row "slop joint" at 115 Nicollet Avenue South. The specials: "Coffee alone" for ten cents; two boiled eggs, bread, butter, and coffee went for thirty-five cents. Courtesy of the City of Minneapolis.

View of the 1953 addition to the Union City Mission, the largest soul-saving complex in the Gateway, at Hennepin Avenue and Second Street. Its pastor, the Reverend William Paul, was dubbed a "builder of men." To the right is Hennepin Avenue, looking north toward the Great Northern Depot. Photograph from City of Minneapolis. Courtesy of the Hennepin History Museum.

It takes a special kind of pastor to preach at a mission. One of them, a Norwegian immigrant named Marie Sandvik, was called to the Gateway after a repentant prostitute told her what it was like there. She bought an old bar at 121 Nicollet, converted it into the Minneapolis Revival Mission, and set about drying men out and setting them right. The men of the Gateway could expect no coddling from the likes of the Reverend William E. Paul, general superintendent of the Union City Mission for an astonishing thirty-six years. Paul was a towering figure among the Gateway's missionaries, and he had an institution to match his stature. Founded in 1895 by a coalition of

MISSIONS

Protestant churches, the Union City Mission ran a virtual skyscraper of a hotel, the twelve-story, "fireproof" St. James, built in 1916 on Second Street North. The mission's more modern outpost on Hennepin Avenue, built in 1953 adjacent to the St. James, was topped with three crosses, a reference to Calvary, where two thieves, one bound for heaven, the other hell, died on crosses with Jesus. Outside the city, Paul created Mission Farms to put the idle to work tilling fields by the shores of Medicine Lake. The main mission fed a thousand mouths a day, had sleeping room for five hundred, and offered the Gateway District's only delousing unit. It was said to be the largest rescue mission in the United States.

With a spiritual rehab complex sprawling from the city's streets to the farm fields, Paul was dubbed a "rebuilder of men," someone who could construct "new bodies and new ambitions out of the old and broken clay." But in his view, some of those men were busted beyond repair. You could see that by the meal tickets the mission distributed to panhandlers instead of spare change that could be spent on rotgut liquor. The cover of the ticket book carried a number of pointers for the mission volunteers who handed out the tickets:

> Don't give your money for moonshine, dope or support
> of a man too lazy to work
> Expert Beggars Require Expert Treatment
> Let the Union City Mission sift the needy and deserving
> from the professional beggar, tramp or crook
> Ample facilities to feed and house the deserving
> Cheaper and better
> If we refuse to help a man there's a reason

Johnny Rex did not attribute any moral superiority to those who professed to sort out the deserving from the depraved. When I asked him about the missions, he told me only about one of them, a place whose name he did not remember, but he did recall it was run by two mean sisters. They raised money by traveling from church to church in Minnesota, making a persuasive pitch for their missionary work but keeping enough of the proceeds to afford a forty-thousand-dollar house, costly real estate for the time. "They lived like queens," he said.

He made a point of telling me they conducted their fund-raising at Lutheran, not Catholic, churches (Johnny was raised Catholic). He did not think much of their attitude toward drinkers, either. During the mission services, if they smelled alcohol on one of the gandy dancers, they would pinch him under the arm. "Get out get out get out get out," the sisters would yell, as they frog-marched the unfortunate drunk out the door of God's house. I doubt Johnny ever observed this behavior. He probably heard about it secondhand from his guys. I am sure that in his line of work, he had little patience for those who lacked hospitality for practicing alcoholics.

Working undercover, sociology graduate student William Eckland witnessed a similar ejection during an evening service at the Harbor Light mission. He counted thirty men in the room one night. Two members of the congregation were fast asleep during the service. Three were "visibly drunk."

> When the regular preacher began to speak, one of the drunks asked, "How can we be saved?" The man at the door told him to be quiet. He kept on yelling. As the group leader said, "If you believe in Christ, then you must live the image of Christ," the worker at the door grabbed the drunk and physically threw him out of the building. As the sermon continued, the leader referred many times to this "other life of sin on the Avenue."

The presence of researchers like Eckland is the only reason we have accounts of the hellfire-and-brimstone sermons or the rough treatment of drunken reprobates. The graduate students dressed like all the other guys, or at least they tried to, but their floppy hats and worn-out shoes were all a disguise. They were young and probably scribbled in notebooks when they thought no one was looking. In its final years, the Gateway was under constant surveillance from researchers obsessed with documenting every detail of its conditions.

Given how long the missions had operated in the Gateway, city leaders may have lost faith that religious organizations could solve the problem. So they placed their hope in social science. In 1958 the Minneapolis Housing and Redevelopment Authority appointed a committee to decide what to do with three thousand men who were in the way of their urban renewal plan. Professor Theodore Caplow, chairman of the University of Minnesota Department of Sociology, worked with the committee to provide some answers. It's still unclear whether this project was merely window dressing for the city's "bum removal program" or a sincere effort to improve the lives of men relocated for the greater good. Nevertheless, a remarkable amount of work went into it. In the spring of 1958, Professor Caplow began an extraordinary research project that would send nine graduate students pretending to be Skid Row residents as participant observers—the term of art for a researcher in the field back then. By the late 1950s, impersonating a Gateway hobo had already been a popular pastime for news reporters, and even some concerned citizens got in on the act. This project went well beyond the one- or two-night slumming of those folks. Wallace described the cast of characters: "One took the role of hobo, another that of an ex-G.I., a third became an alcoholic, a fourth played a variety of roles, and the only woman on the staff became the confidante of a prostitute." Wallace pretended to be a "casual laborer." Their field research lasted four months and produced fourteen hundred single-spaced, typed pages of reportage, called Participant Observation Journals.

When I read about this sheer volume of research data in Wallace's 1965 book, *Skid Row as a Way of Life*, I became obsessed all over again. I had to have those Participant Observation Journals, because no other document, with the exception of Johnny Rex's recollections, home movies, and snapshots, captured the Gateway's final moments in such detail. I found the retired professor Wallace on the East Coast and over the phone gently but firmly prodded him about the journals' whereabouts. Alas, at some point, during one of the many moves in his academic career, they were lost. No one anticipated that someday a journalist in Minnesota would need them. The excerpts in Wallace's book are the only fragments of the journals that remain, as well as the memories of the surviving participants of their four-month expedition. Wallace shared with me some of his unorthodox research techniques.

He had heard rumors that cops often relieved Skid Rowers of their bankrolls as they hauled them off to the drunk tank. The police denied such behavior. Wallace decided to see for himself. He stopped bathing, put on the appropriate Gateway uniform, and tried to get the cops to arrest him for public drunkenness. This ruse presented a quandary, because Wallace could not get so drunk that he was unaware of what was happening to him. He had to drink enough to smell the part, but there was no guarantee that he could keep up the act well enough to persuade a cop to arrest him. He read through the police reports and learned the secret. Pissing himself was a sure ticket to the pokey. So one day, on the streets of his city, Sam Wallace sacrificed his trousers for the sake of sociology.

He told me the rest: "The police promptly picked me up, gently put me in the Black Maria, took me off to the jail, and proceeded to take all the money that I had. It was just a few dollars." Theory proved.

The next day, they took him to court. The judge was in on the game. He gave the "drunk" a "sentence" of ten days in the workhouse, which was the next phase of his research. He had his own cell and served his time without causing any trouble. He had made sure to get booked under a phony name so it wouldn't come back to haunt him in his career.

Another student, Ronald Corwin, disguised himself as a long-distance truck driver with a torn T-shirt, baggy trousers, and worn shoes. This role provided a convenient alibi during his long absences from Skid Row, because he would be "on the road." His objective was to study two hotels in detail. He doesn't remember their names, but he recalls how different they were.

"One was a disgusting, dirty haven for unshaven, shabbily dressed alcoholics, who pooled their limited money to buy cheap wine, which they all shared." Those who could not contribute were pressured to get out. It sounded like the Victor or the Pioneer. The other hotel "catered to aging, retired widowers down on their luck, but struggling to maintain the respect they once enjoyed. They all wore white shirts, ties, and jackets—badly wrinkled and often smudged and yellowing to be sure, but nonetheless worn proudly." Those gentlemen felt bad enough for the young newcomer that they went through garbage cans to find better clothing for him so he would fit the dress code of the faded but still classy hotel. Corwin may have been referring to the Beaufort.

There were so many graduate students working in the Gateway

back then that Corwin said, "On quiet days we sometimes found our-selves in the embarrassing position of observing each other." Corwin felt guilty about his deception, and when the project was all over, he went back and confessed to the men. Nevertheless, Corwin thought the motives of Professor Caplow were pure and that there was a real community in the Gateway worth relocating somewhere else.

Michael Rockland, an American studies graduate student who signed up because he needed the money, saw the project's motives differently. He remembers being dispatched to the Lower Loop to find out where these guys were going to move, in case a critical mass of residents ended up establishing a new Skid Row somewhere else. He put on his "scuzziest" clothes, and while he didn't particularly like the job, he recalled with pride that none of the authentic Gateway characters caught on to his deceit. At that time, his wife was at home with a newborn, and Rockland worried about infecting them with tuberculosis that he might pick up from living on Skid Row.

The most involved of all the researchers must have been graduate student Keith Lovald. Though he didn't put on a disguise, Lovald worked directly for the city as the coordinator of the whole research project. Lovald also used his research to produce a brick of a disser-tation that weighs in at 484 pages and is perhaps the most exhaus-tive report on the Gateway's Skid Row days. It also reveals just how zealously Lovald embraced his job, tallying facts about a place and a people, to the point of obsession.

In September 1959, Lovald got a room in the Washington Hotel, with a bird's-eye view of the intersection of Washington and Mar-quette Avenues. His mission: clandestine surveillance. His target: panhandlers. He wielded a camera with a telephoto lens, and his partner took notes as he related what he saw and photographed. The target came into view, a drunken fellow, about forty-five years old, wearing filthy and wrinkled clothes that looked as if he had slept in them. His first panhandle occurred just outside Johnny's Sourdough Bar, at 8:25 a.m. He got nothing. He moved down Washington Ave-nue, stopping to beg in front of Hughes Liquors, the Gay Nineties Tavern, and the Marquette Tavern. Lovald snapped a photo of each attempted panhandle and dutifully recorded the time. He followed the man for ninety-six minutes. Hiding in that hotel room, Lovald and his notetaker kept at it for another eight and a half hours, adding another eighteen panhandlers to their life list. Out on the street, they recorded the panhandler's scripts: "Can you spare a dime for a bowl of soup?" "Spare a dime for an old Swede?" "Will you buy a memorial picture of Floyd Olson? Only 25 cents."

Lovald was nothing if not detail-oriented. Long after Caplow's graduate students had burned their Skid Row clothing and gone back to class, Lovald was still working the Gateway. In what must have been a vile task, in May 1959, he counted the number of plumbing facilities that served the three thousand men of the Gateway (82 bathtubs, 84 showers, 220 toilets, and 75 urinals). He counted the number of double-breasted suits in one secondhand store on Third Street South (4,700). He estimated the percentage of patrons of the Gateway's thirty-three bars who were visibly inebriated (33 percent). He counted the percentage of mission beds reserved for the night's converts that remained vacant (usually 100 percent). He followed the men on their wanderings to Elliot Park and Loring Park or to the jungle down by the Mississippi River, where the hoboes waited to hop freight trains to Milwaukee and Chicago or the West Coast. He spied on the men sleeping in old truck bodies underneath the Stone Arch Bridge and watched them gather water from the springs bubbling from the limestone riverbank.

Johnny Rex was underwhelmed with the university students' scholarship, however. After reading one report, he thought, "Shit, they don't know any more than the guy who went to the bathroom."

Six frames from a researcher's camera show the progress of a Gateway panhandler at work. Keith Lovald, a University of Minnesota sociology student, got a room at the Washington Hotel and pointed his telephoto lens out the window across Washington Avenue. The arrows point out the panhandler, who starts his mostly unsuccessful journey in front of the Sourdough Bar. From Keith A. Lovald, "From Hobohemia to Skid Row: The Changing Community of the Homeless Man" (PhD diss., University of Minnesota, 1960).

8:25 a.m.   8:26 a.m.

8:28 a.m.   8:28 a.m.

8:29 - 8:55 a.m.   8:55 - 9:51 a.m.

By the time he handed in his dissertation in May 1960, Lovald noted that urban renewal had already scattered a third of the Gateway's population. For someone who counted urinals but never identified a single Gateway resident by name, he sounded a more human note at the end of his tome: "It should not be forgotten that a bulldozer and a sledgehammer cannot destroy a community in the same way that its buildings are demolished. Minneapolis, as is true of any large city, has a need for a place where the impoverished, the disesteemed, and the powerless can take refuge and find comfort."

A little over two years later, a familiar tune floated out over Hennepin Avenue from the loudspeaker of the Union City Mission. By this time, it had become clear that the mission could not escape the spreading waters of the urban renewal flood. On December 10, 1962, the old hymn summoned the men for a final Christmas dinner.

> Are you washed in the blood,
> In the soul-cleansing blood of the Lamb?
> Are your garments spotless? Are they white as snow?
> Are you washed in the blood of the Lamb?

Inside, men with garments that were somewhat less than spotless feasted on donated cookies, coffee cake, pastries, and fifty dollars worth of candy. They belted out Christmas carols that must have echoed through the emptying halls. Dead since 1955, Reverend Paul wasn't around to see it. Watching over them was his replacement, a wistful Reverend Claude Moore.

Five months after the Christmas party, the Union City Mission was vacant. A reporter who visited found rows of empty green plastic-covered chairs in the St. James lobby, and on the deserted clerk's desk, a few lilac blossoms wilting in a water glass. The mission had tried to rebuild men for nearly seventy years, but now the city's mission to rebuild the neighborhood made no distinction between the purveyors of sin and those who tried to reform the sinners. All of it was part of the problem, and all of it would go.

"We've seen more adult tears in the past three months," the reverend told a reporter from the *Minneapolis Star*. "One man said he'd never leave. He did. They found him in the river last week."

Reuben Larson, pastor of the Gateway Gospel Mission,
35 Washington Avenue South, stands on a chair in the gutter in
a ceremony marking the end of the mission's work saving souls
there, June 1961. "Skid Row is smashed, the men have scattered,"
he said. Photograph by Pete Hohn, *Minneapolis Star Tribune.*
Courtesy of the Minnesota Historical Society.

═ 6 ═

THE LOST CITY

On a December afternoon in Minneapolis in 2011, Johnny Rex sat in his TV room with his body cradled in an easy chair. His legs were elevated on a footrest, and they looked too thin to hold him up. Resting on the wooden armrests, his hands seemed to move about on their own accord, as if they were compensating for the involuntary immobility of his other limbs. The side of his neck was a landscape of ridges and valleys, and one tract pulsated almost violently. He had aged dramatically since I first met him in person two years earlier, though I was surprised then that he was still alive. He may have been equally surprised to have lasted this long, for he was a man who kept track of all of his brushes with death, each bout of food poisoning, a near drowning as a toddler, the stray police bullet that zipped past his ear, the two bypass surgeries, a blood clot, a heart attack, colon cancer, the lightning strike while he was swimming, getting thrown through the roof of a Nash after it crashed, a blow to the head from a golf ball that knocked him out cold for ten minutes. The "deathly incidents" numbered twenty-two in all, including fifty-eight months in the military during World War II, but he had tallied that list a decade earlier, and it looked to me as if this time, the Grim Reaper wasn't going to take a rain check.

He apologized for being fuzzy, which he blamed on the pain pill that he had just taken to ease the agony of his collapsing vertebrae. He shouldn't have been in Minneapolis at all that December day, because every winter since the 1960s had been spent on an island in the Gulf of Mexico, shooting the breeze with the regulars on the docks at Anna Maria. Nine months earlier, he had tripped on a curb coming out of a jewelry store, and it was as if he had never stopped falling. He made it up north for the summer, but wasn't well enough to head back before the snows came. In a way I was lucky he was still in town, because it gave me another chance to pull a few more stories out of him. So I asked him about the fire, and he recalled it like it happened yesterday.

On a hot summer night in 1961, Johnny Rex arrived at the Sourdough Bar and found himself in the midst of chaos. A fire had broken out in the back of the saloon, and now it threatened to burn down the entire block. The other two businesses in the old building, the Senate Café and the Senate Hotel, were both in flames. Firefighters clambered up ladders that reached to the third floor, where smoke was pouring out of the windows. The rescuers scrambled through the hallways, looking for flophouse tenants who couldn't get out on their own. They found a man who was deaf and mute, full of smoke, and got him out. Another one was pulled out and laid on the sidewalk, where a firefighter held an oxygen mask to his face to save his ravaged lungs. Behind the two men, the rescuer and the victim, the colossal foaming goblet painted on the storefront of the Sourdough Bar beckoned, as always, though this time, no one was serving.

It didn't take much to attract a crowd in the Gateway, so a four-alarm fire naturally brought out hundreds of spectators, and with traffic blocked off and people running every which way, Washington Avenue South became an unruly carnival. I'm sure everyone thought this might be the big one, the Sodom-smiting blaze that would race through the decaying buildings and reduce Skid Row to a smoking heap. Maybe that was what they wanted, because the throngs were making things tough for the rescue squads. Some of the jostling

In July 1961, a Minneapolis firefighter administers oxygen to a smoke-poisoned resident of the Senate Hotel, 34 Washington Avenue South. The Sourdough Bar is in the background. Photograph by Pete Hohn, *Minneapolis Star Tribune*. Courtesy of the Minnesota Historical Society.

bystanders kept stepping on the hoses and impeding the flow of water. The cops finally got fed up and carried two hose-stompers off to jail.

The firefighters recognized Johnny when he got there, and they were happy to see him. He was a supporter of the Minneapolis Fire Department, lending his building for union meetings and allowing posters in his storefront when the union was lobbying the city for a raise. Now they wanted to return the favor. The ranking firefighter on the scene made him an offer: "John, you want us to put it out, or let it burn a little bit?"

As Johnny watched his beloved bar go up in flames, it must have seemed that his life was going up in smoke. His marriage had already been on the rocks when his young wife died that spring, her body ruined by hepatitis and alcoholism, leaving him a single father with five children. As if that weren't enough, he found out he could be headed to jail. A grand jury was investigating Minneapolis's notoriously corrupt liquor license system and decided that Johnny had violated the erratically enforced law that limited individuals to one liquor establishment each. Of course he had, but so had everybody else. Just about every major player in the liquor business, including aldermen and notorious gangsters, was accused of hiding their liquor empires behind shell companies and aging relatives. Even if he did beat the rap, Johnny was watching buildings falling to rubble all around him, as the city moved forward in its determination to wipe out Skid Row, once and for all. Sooner or later the wrecking ball would come to his block of Washington Avenue, and transferring a liquor license to another part of town would be a daunting task, even without a criminal charge hanging over him. Perhaps he could have walked away and started again somewhere else.

Johnny was a soft touch for a handout to a drunk in need, but a hardheaded businessman in the end. The decision about whether to let his bar burn came down to dollars and cents. He had no insurance on the Sourdough, so he had everything to lose if the place burned to the ground. "Put it out," he commanded. The firefighters aimed their cannons and the waters erupted forth. If anyone thought the proprietor of the Sourdough Bar would go quietly, they were wrong.

The fire investigators said it started in a couple of barrels of fuel

A carnival scene broke out on Washington Avenue as firefighters
worked the blaze at the Senate Hotel and Sourdough Bar. Johnny
said the firefighters gave him the option of letting it burn. He
turned them down. Photograph by Pete Hohn, *Minneapolis Star
Tribune.* Courtesy of the Minnesota Historical Society.

oil in the back of the bar, but Johnny thought this was no accident. In that neighborhood, fires didn't just start by themselves. He was sure his former clerk, one-legged Larson, the guy who loved to watch people suffer, was behind it. Of course he couldn't prove it. So he put his head down, hired people to fix the damage, and before long reopened for business. Soon the bell was clanging at the Sourdough Bar, and the gandy dancers on Washington Avenue rejoiced.

The party went on for four months. Then the letter Johnny had dreaded finally came. You have three days to close up, it said. Three days.

On the last night, in early December 1961, everybody showed up. The word was out on Skid Row that the bell was ringing all night at the Sourdough. The place turned into a madhouse. It was the kind of night that could make people forget their world was falling down around them. Men in fedoras jostling, women laughing with their heads thrown back, bartenders scrambling, glasses clinking and beer and cocktails pouring down throats, smoke from dozens of cigarettes curling into the air, and above it all, someone perched high above the bar, filming the last night of the Sourdough for all eternity.

Then it was over. Johnny tacked up hand-painted signs on the plywood storefronts of the Sourdough, one over the foaming beer goblet, the other over the giant 10. "Closed forever!" they said, with an exclamation point flourish. A *Minneapolis Tribune* photographer stopped by to document the aftermath, and shot an image of a despondent-looking fellow, hands jammed in the pockets of his dark overcoat, a dark cap on his head, walking past the closed bar without looking at it. It could be Johnny, but it's hard to tell, he's so bundled up. In the photograph, the sign for the Senate Hotel is still there, with the price of rooms ("50¢ and up") so predictable that it is a permanent part of the marquee. Down at the end of the block and across Marquette, where the Purity Liquor Store once stood, only a pile of rubble remains.

The Sourdough was Johnny's last foothold in a Skid Row that was rapidly falling into oblivion. The city had declared war on the Gateway, and the Minneapolis Housing and Redevelopment Authority would not be satisfied with anything less than obliteration. The

Drinks were on the house on the last night at the Sourdough Bar in December 1961. The scene was probably shot by a University of Minnesota film student, Rod Lazorik, and stitched into Johnny's movie. From the film *Skidrow*. Courtesy of John and Barbara Bacich.

buildings were so infested that they were beyond rescue, according to city inspectors. "They state that rats have, through the 75 or 100 years in the life of old buildings, burrowed holes from one building to another so that the rat can travel for blocks. The frame and soft mortar walls make it possible for rats to travel through the upper floors." The rats were left to their own devices when it came to finding a new place to live. But to get rid of 186 buildings in the "redevelopment area," the HRA would have to empty them of people first. As of 1958, when the demolition really got rolling, about three thousand people lived in the area. The vast majority were single men, which in

In December 1961, a sign on the Sourdough Bar tells
Washington Avenue that the place is closed forever. Johnny's
effort to transfer his on-sale license ran into trouble with city
aldermen. The view is east on Washington Avenue South.
Photograph by Earl Seubert. Copyright Star Tribune Media
Company LLC. Reprinted with permission.

the 1950s presented a significant advantage from a cost perspective. Under federal law, single men and transients were not entitled to any money to help find them a new place to live. These kinds of people were expected to fend for themselves. The HRA felt the policy was perhaps too harsh and that it owed something to people thrown out of their homes, however squalid they were, so it set up a relocation office. If the men found a new place to live and came back to the office with proof, they could get five bucks. The agency's larger ambition to build housing for these men fell victim to Skid Row's toxic reputation. The HRA identified potential locations for that new housing, which would consist of single-room occupancy units and some communal facilities, just like the men were used to. But every site they proposed sparked such violent opposition that they gave up and went looking for a new one. It happened nine times before a last-ditch effort to build the housing project downtown was vetoed by the city council. The city of Minneapolis would hand out five-dollar bills and advice to whoever asked, but it wasn't about to help Skid Row sprout all over again.

As the inhabitants of Skid Row scattered to Seven Corners, North Washington Avenue, Nicollet Avenue South, and points beyond, the institutions of Skid Row vanished with even less ceremony. It started with the Vendome Hotel, on Fourth Street, and spread north, west, and east, consuming what had been the Milner Hotel, the Allan Hotel, Walter's Bar, Rusciano Restaurant, Pioneer Square Bar, Nate's Clothing, Silver Dollar Bar, Moler Barber College, Bijou Theater, Ciresi's Liquor Store, the Phoenix Building, the Kasota Building, the Grand Theater, the Janney, Semple & Hill Warehouse, the Persian Palms, the Great Lakes Bar, and dozens and dozens of other businesses and missions and theaters and beer joints, a massive and total eradication of the old city, the scale of which would never be possible today. Punched by the wrecking ball, buildings that had stood for seventy or more years crumbled like sandcastles. Johnny stood on the sidewalk with his movie camera, watching Skid Row finally succumb. In his film, there is one building that could be the Victor Hotel, but two of the four walls are gone, and now the windows are just gaping holes. "You could see how fast these buildings came down,"

Johnny said, "because there was no steel in them. Just wood and brick. All they had to do was swing that big old bucket and barely hit it, and it would fall down."

A few years later, a city brochure exulted in the demolition's supposed success. "Taverns and pawnshops are gone. . . . The dark, dirty, traffic-choked streets and alleys are gone; new pavement, modern bright street lights and adequate off-street parking for today's and tomorrow's needs are here. . . . The rat-infested bottle-lined alleys are gone; tree-lined and grassed pedestrian areas are making them a thing of the past." The photograph above it shows a block of Washington Avenue, including the Sourdough Bar, with a blue squiggle on it, meaning that it had been scratched from existence with the ease of a pen stroke.

Johnny took some of his favorite gandies with him—Jim Headley, the survivor; Jim Shelley, the former Marine; a hard worker named Frankie Antolik—and set them up in a rooming house he bought on Washington Avenue North. Relocating his liquor business was not so easy. He was convinced that the "schlocky crooks" in the HRA treated him poorly because he refused to bribe them. He no longer had the threat of prison hanging over him—a judge had thrown out the liquor cases en masse that September—but the city council was still waffling about letting Johnny transfer the license from the Sourdough to anywhere else in Minneapolis. Someone brought up the old claim that it was a breeding ground for venereal disease. The council had reluctantly let him open a new liquor store nine blocks away, at 1118 Hennepin. Johnny told me he bought it from the Syndicate, the liquor monopoly controlled by Kid Cann and his more temperate brother, Harry Bloom, whom Johnny considered a friend. He had no illusion his future was in selling booze, but he wasn't sure exactly what his future was. Johnny put it this way: "Contrary to what people thought when I got off Skid Row, I didn't have a pot to urinate in and I didn't have a window to throw it out of."

He wasn't the only one. Mike Skavene, another liquor store owner and former bootlegger, had made enough enemies among Minneapolis's corrupt liquor interests that he found his license relocated from the Gateway (the Bowery Liquor Store) to a nearly deserted

The wrecking ball goes to work on the building housing
Rex Liquors and the A&C Hotel. Nicollet Avenue South is
in the foreground, looking north. Photograph from City of
Minneapolis. Courtesy of the Hennepin History Museum.

industrial area west of downtown. With few customers in the area, Skavene was struggling to pay the rent. One day, he told his landlord, Abraham Bloom, he had had enough and that they should come by and do an inventory, take what they wanted, and let him get on with his life. Frank Wolinski, recently departed from the city council but still waist deep in liquor deals, found someone to take over the business. So on a September morning in 1962, the fixer and the landlord arranged to meet with Skavene at the store. About 8:30 a.m., Johnny got a call from Wolinski, asking if he could come by and help with the inventory. No, Johnny said. His father-in-law was in the hospital for an operation, so he had to be there. "That's what saved my life," John told me. As the day went on, Skavene sat glumly while the men who would take over his business went through the store, counting up the remaining bottles of booze. Skavene said he was going out for lunch. When he got back, his landlord asked one last time about the back rent. Wolinski had just arrived when Skavene pulled out a revolver, muttered something, and shot him through the neck. His landlord ran for the door, screaming, "Don't, don't, don't." Skavene fired two bullets into Bloom's back. He left the two men bleeding among the bottles, got in his Cadillac Coupe, and drove off aimlessly through the city. Word quickly spread, and everyone who had anything to do with Skavene's business travails—the city inspectors, the gangsters, the aldermen—thought they were next. All of them left town at high speed. They were safe, it turned out. Six hours after the bloodshed in the liquor store, the police found Skavene about a mile from his house, behind the wheel of his 1956 Caddy, fast asleep.

Bloom was dead. Wolinski, the old fighter, survived. Wearing a neck brace, he testified against Skavene at trial, and while the store owner was shipped off to Stillwater prison, not even a bullet in the neck could dissuade Wolinski from remaining city hall's fixer on all things liquor.

Johnny Rex may not have had a pot to piss in, but he had something far more valuable. He called it his "real estate eye." Pretty soon he would have plenty of windows, and they would be full of beer and liquor signs flashing neon. The real money came not from peddling liquor but from owning the buildings where the precious licenses

10_283

11 21 60

Its shelves empty of booze, the old Rex Liquors at 201 Nicollet in November 1960 still displays posters advertising Cream of Kentucky bourbon. Johnny managed to transfer the liquor license to a new location on Hennepin Avenue. Courtesy of the City of Minneapolis.

allowed liquor to be sold. He had watched aldermen play this game for years, so now he was determined to do it himself. In 1964 he sold Rex Liquors and never peddled a bottle of booze again. His friendship with Wolinski, who orchestrated the real estate deals, paid off handsomely. Within a decade, Johnny was worth more than one million dollars, with residential and commercial properties across south Minneapolis. What eluded him, still, was his reputation. In 1974 he stood to gain when Wolinski finally prevailed in his twenty-year crusade to eliminate the old patrol limits and open up the rest of the city to liquor businesses. He learned that the city's love-hate relationship with the bottle lingered on.

In 1976 Johnny picked up a copy of the *Minneapolis Tribune* and found himself, and his business, on the front page. His success as a landlord for liquor outlets was an object of scrutiny. A liquor store owner, Bob Peterson, told the reporter that he paid Johnny twelve thousand dollars a year in rent and picked up the taxes, too. "He'll squeeze you till you're dead, then take your fillings." In his interview with the *Tribune*, Johnny said that he felt similar pressure when he was in Peterson's shoes, but from the wholesalers, and that's why he decided to become a landlord.

"A hard-nosed businessman? I don't mind being called that. I take it as a compliment. A lot of people call me a dumb Polack, and that doesn't bother me either."

Later that year, he picked up the paper again, and this time he hit the roof. Johnny was caught up once again in a Minneapolis police investigation involving the illegal ownership of multiple liquor licenses. Johnny and his friend Wolinski were accused of filing a fraudulent liquor license application. Then the police showed up at the door of

Neither political setbacks, indictments, nor a bullet in the neck deterred Frank Wolinski from making a livelihood in Minneapolis's liquor business. In 1976, long out of office, he remained the fixer for liquor licenses. Photograph by Bruce Bisping, *Minneapolis Star Tribune*. Courtesy of the Minnesota Historical Society.

NEW
Wolinski
POST EXCLUSIVE!
North Minneapolis
Post Finds 35th District Vote
LIQUOR PATROL LIMITS
MINNEAPOLIS, MINNESOTA

Johnny's house on Harriet Avenue, waving a search warrant. They left with all kinds of papers that they used to accuse Wolinski of theft and perjury in the manipulation of liquor licenses. The charges never stuck. John didn't get charged with anything and thought about suing the newspaper for defamation. Down in Florida, he was the darling of the docks, a philanthropist and the social chair, but back in Minneapolis, Johnny just couldn't shake the taint of making a living in the world of alcohol.

Something was changing in Minneapolis, though. For all its high-minded plans and purple prose, the new Gateway turned out to be as lifeless as the old one was lively. The 1950s vision of blocky towers and wide boulevards and concrete parking lots had killed off street life almost entirely, and some of the modern architectural marvels quickly fell into obsolescence. The Sheraton-Ritz Hotel didn't even last thirty years before it was knocked back into a surface parking lot in 1990, which has remained that way ever since. People mourned the loss of a landmark that was collateral damage from the Gateway redevelopment: the magnificent Metropolitan Building, the first sky-scraper west of the Mississippi when it was finished in 1890 with a soaring light court in its interior that made it a true marvel of engineering and design. Like the neighborhood around it, it was falling apart after years of shoddy maintenance, and despite a spirited effort to save it that went to the Minnesota Supreme Court, the Housing and Redevelopment Authority prevailed in its decision to demolish it. The loss was regretted almost immediately, and it had a similar effect in Minneapolis that the destruction of Penn Station brought in New York City, spurring a civic resolve to preserve old buildings whenever possible.

Minneapolis was coming to realize what it had lost. In 1978 David Rosheim published *The Other Minneapolis*, the first history of the neighborhood. The book drew on Rosheim's fascination with the place as a teenager who took a train to the big city and got his first glimpse of Skid Row at the very end of its existence. He was haunted by the "recurring dream landscape, the sunset Washington Avenue of grim wine-red skies, the interminable avenue of despair." That description sounds much more soulful than its replacement when

Rosheim returned after the demolitions: "An aerial view of the Gateway looks like a huge used car lot with tall buildings placed here and there randomly." Rosheim found out about Johnny, who was more than willing to share his tales, such as a check swindle carried out by the bartender on drunken patrons at Harry Smull's Persian Palms, the joint across the street from the Sourdough. Rosheim presented the Gateway as much more than a collection of bums—over the years, it was a center of political intrigue, violence, sexual freedom, radical politics, entertainment, debauchery, yes, but also everything that made a city interesting. Writing in 1989, two professors at the University of Minnesota could still describe the Gateway project as "a bold planning effort on the part of Minneapolis," but they also noted that in Seattle, the city that gave Skid Row its name, the old Pioneer Square neighborhood was revitalized and now attracted squadrons of tourists who milled around the old rusticated buildings. "Perhaps the same thing could have been done in Minneapolis," they wrote.

Meanwhile, Johnny, who belonged to every veterans group you could name and a good bunch of other ones, was always the life of the party when he set up the projector and threaded the color film that had been stitched together by the students at the University of Minnesota so many years earlier. He carted his reel of celluloid to the Moose Lodge, the Elks, the Rotarians, the VFW, the inmates at Stillwater prison. He got tired of talking over the rattling movie projector every time, so in about 1986 someone showed him how to record a voice-over to accompany the half-hour film.

The film begins with one word, *SKIDROW*, in white letters on a black background. Then the voice comes on, rough as exposed brick, a northern Minnesota brogue that's part Scandinavian, part Slavic, all sincere. "My name is John Bacich, and I took this film, about Skid Row down on Washington Avenue in Minneapolis, so that people could see what it was all about in the late 1950s. This film now is twenty-six years old, unrehearsed, and I'm sure you're going to enjoy it." The scenes that followed are now an indelible part of Minnesota history.

In 1998 Johnny's film, accompanied by a half-hour modern documentary about the neighborhood, was broadcast on public television and instantly made John Bacich a minor celebrity. The documentary filmmaker, John Lightfoot, filmed Johnny sitting on a bar stool, walking over the Stone Arch Bridge, or standing in front of the former location of his bar, now an insurance office modeled after the Parthenon and designed by Minoru Yamasaki, the man behind the World Trade Center. Suddenly Johnny was featured in the newspaper as a witness to history, a caretaker of wayward old men, a chronicler of a neighborhood wiped out by arrogance and shortsightedness. After I met Johnny, he mailed me a DVD with his movie on it, and an accompanying flyer describing it. Then he sent it to me again, and again, and once more, and I probably have five copies in my file cabinet. His home movies gave him a legitimacy that he always sought, and in his later years, he reveled in it.

Curiously, for all his efforts documenting the Gateway, Johnny Rex does not count himself among those revisionists who think the city should have left it standing. In fact, he sometimes sounded like he would have torched the Sourdough Bar himself, if the numbers worked. I asked him once if Minneapolis made a mistake by wrecking Skid Row. He barely let me finish the question. "No, no. Hell no. It was a firetrap, nothing but bums. No taxes. How could the city support it when there were no taxes?"

His home movie has become a cult favorite in the Twin Cities. It has been rebroadcast over and over, and it is regularly screened in art houses in the Twin Cities. In August 2011, a film lover named Peter Schilling left a showing at the Trylon microcinema in south Minneapolis, his mind blown, just as mine is every time I see it. He wrote on his blog that he was moved by the experience delivered by "a humble storyteller of the finest vintage." "The shots are, simply put, incredible. Their composition, the vibrant color, and the often startling images of these troubled drunks strains credibility—it amazes me that after six showings in three days that a guy can shoot some home movies over a few years that a perfect stranger such as myself would watch in a heartbeat over *Citizen Kane*.

"Thank you, Johnny Bacich, wherever you are . . ."

At that moment, Johnny was likely immobile in his home on Harriet Avenue, maybe looking out the window to the blooming

John Bacich poses for a photographer in what used to be the
heart of Skid Row, now a collection of modernist buildings,
plazas, and parking lots. When his film was broadcast statewide
in 1998, he gained a legitimacy that had long eluded him in
Minneapolis. Photograph by Cheryl Diaz Meyer. Copyright Star
Tribune Media Company LLC. Reprinted with permission.

garden out back, listening to the birds at the feeder, maybe wondering when that writer who wouldn't leave him alone would ride his bicycle over and talk more about the old days.

I came as often as I could, which is to say, not as much as I needed or wanted to. Still, by the time I showed up at his house in October 2012, I had interviewed him twenty-five times. I felt I barely knew him, but it was getting harder for him to generate the momentum that kept the stories flowing. He was propped in his usual spot that afternoon, and confessed to aching for twenty-four hours straight. I watched him as he spoke. His jaw looked uneven and shaky as he washed down some pills with a glass of water. He munched slowly on a raisin bran muffin, something that appeared to take quite an effort.

Still, once I got him going, he talked about the "weird psycho" that he was convinced had torched the Sourdough. He boasted about serving eight ounces of beer in a glass that should have held twelve, how he once put up sixty-seven men in his flophouse, some of whom crashed on the old thrift store couches, and the bell over the bar that rang and rang and rang and rang and rang, free drinks for everybody.

"Get the hell out of here for five minutes," Johnny said to me. That would give him time to take a leak. I told him he could take a lot longer, because I had to be on my way. When I left, his wife and daughter were helping him to his feet. I would never talk to him again.

A week or so later, he got up again, and fell. On his way down his arm hit a piece of furniture. It ripped a gash in the brittle skin, and when he landed on the floor, his hip fractured. He got to the hospital, and they sewed him up. But that was the last injury. They sent him home with a bucket of painkillers that still couldn't stop the hurt. Johnny gave up eating; then he wouldn't drink anything. On November 25, 2012, at ninety-three years, seven months, and nine days of age, he went to sleep and never woke up.

On my way to the Church of the Annunciation a week later, I passed by his home, and its garden, brown and withered in the late autumn, and the Starbucks where I first met him, surrounded by his guys. I walked through the church door. It almost caught me by surprise, the casket in the foyer, open for everyone to see. The mortician had rouged Johnny's cheeks and clumped a lot of waxy clay to straighten his nose. He had glasses over the closed lids of his eyes. His mouth looked too long, the opening betraying the slump of his flesh that would be totally slack without the skill of the embalming technician. His greenish hands clutched a rosary. I saw his wife slip an envelope into the coffin before it was closed. I did not ask her what was inside it.

I went home after the funeral, opened the door to the study, and sat down at my desk. I opened the box of ragged snapshots of gandy dancers and held them in my hand. I remembered how Johnny told me that after his film was shown on television, he started to get phone calls from strangers. They all asked the same kind of question. My uncle, my grandfather, my cousin was on Skid Row back in the 1950s. Did you know him? Do you have a picture of him? Do you know what happened to him? Johnny would look through his gandy family album, and try to remember. He would answer their questions, if he could, because he understood their need to know what happened. The men were all dead, had to be, and these images were probably all that was left of them.

Barbara told me that a few days before his death, Johnny did something very strange. He woke up in the middle of the night and started talking a blue streak about the old days. Out of his mouth came the names of a crooked alderman, a cop, then a name that Barbara didn't recognize. His brain was playing reruns, reliving the desperate and wild days, which were so glorious when he thought of them now, the time he could strut down the street with the gandy dancers walking backward and asking for a dollar, when he could grab his camera and be sure something was happening on Washington Avenue. No one would recognize that Minneapolis anymore, and maybe it's just as well. "It's the middle of the night," Barbara told the King of Skid Row. "Go to sleep." And he did.

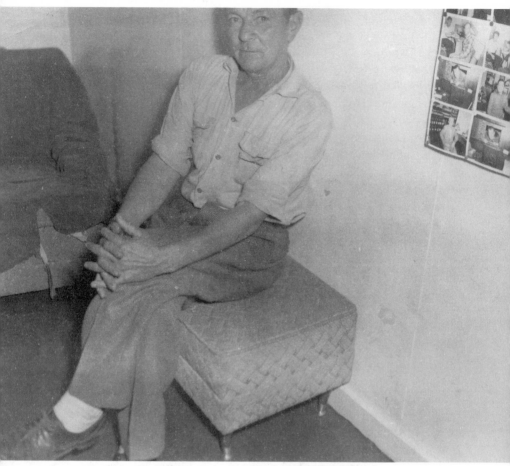

When this man sat for his portrait, those who came before him were already pinned to the wall. His name, like the community that sustained him, is lost to history. Courtesy of John and Barbara Bacich.

≡ Epilogue ≡

On a sunny Saturday morning in July 2014, Hennepin Avenue was waking up from its weekly hangover. Several hours earlier, the hordes of clubbers who had arrived in a cloud of perfume and cologne left in a haze of pepper spray, the preferred tool of the Minneapolis police for sending drunken crowds home at bar close. At 10 a.m., the wide sidewalks were sticky, but mostly deserted. My wife and I stood on the west side of the 400 block of Hennepin, home to Augie's topless bar, the World Famous Brass Rail saloon, a small and furtive-looking porno shop, and the Gay Nineties nightclub, a refugee from the Gateway whose opaque exterior conceals a labyrinth of connected bars and dance floors.

We had chosen this spot for a Gateway promenade, organized by Preserve Minneapolis as part of its summer schedule of historic walking tours. I wanted to start here because it seemed to me that this block, more than any other remaining in the city, felt like the Gateway. The buildings had a certain sag to them, as if their layers upon layers of paint were the only thing holding them up. The businesses inside attracted a mostly hipster-free, hard-bitten, and sometimes homeless clientele. Not that we had any plans to check them out. Our tour participants gathered in front of the little fence that marked the edge of the Gay Nineties sidewalk seating. Behind the barrier, a few Gay Nineties customers sat down at the outdoor tables, starting their weekend morning with longneck Buds and cigarettes.

I started the tour by advising the group that this was as close to the old Skid Row as they would get. They would have to use their imaginations for the rest of the trip, because aside from concrete surfaces and blank walls, there was really nothing to see. I had barely started my spiel when one of the customers stood up, leaned against the barrier, and asked what we were doing. He was tall, lean, maybe in his fifties, dressed in jeans and a sweatshirt. His name, I would learn in a few minutes, was André. Once he heard what we were doing, André smiled broadly and started to add his commentary, loud enough that I was having trouble finishing a sentence. "Yeah, that's right. . . . Skid Row, really? . . . Are you talking about me?"

After a few awkward moments, André went back to his Bud, and we moved down the sidewalk to start our tour; I stood in the landscape of nowhere and tried to evoke the spirit of Johnny Rex. At the corner where Rex Liquors once stood, not only is the building gone but the street as well, replaced by a tennis court. A parking lot and a grassy strip is where the Victor Hotel was, and the then-empty reflecting pool of the insurance company gathered dead leaves where the moving marquee bulbs of the Sourdough Bar once lit up the night.

As it turned out, the blight of the Gateway did not simply relocate to another part of town, the way the aldermen and neighborhood activists had feared. It did something worse. The trouble popped up everywhere. For years afterward, the newspapers declared that the last vestige of Skid Row was coming down, and they were always wrong. Nearly three decades after the city leaders gathered outside the Vendome Hotel to start the Gateway demolition, the next generation of city leaders stood before several hundred people on the 600 block of Hennepin announcing the demolition of another blighted area. The target was the notorious "Block E," a string of peep show parlors, porno bookstores, and dive bars like Moby Dick's, home of the "whale of a drink." On that October day in 1988, the community members released balloons and sang songs to celebrate the demolition of six old buildings and their replacement with a parking lot. The city ultimately paid $39 million to build the new Block E, a faux suburban shopping mall transplanted on the Hennepin strip. It lasted barely a decade before falling into its own obsolescence.

The mission shelters remain in downtown Minneapolis, at the

Salvation Army, the House of Charity, and Mary's Place, allowing the forlorn and the desperate to sleep in the shadow of the big sports arenas. The demolition of the Gateway did take the last cubicle hotel out of service. Yet its modern counterpart is the "wet house." These are government-funded versions of what Johnny and his fellow flophouse proprietors provided subsidy free: a safe place for alcoholics to live without having to embrace sobriety. Catholic Charities operates a wet house that provides eighty apartments for "late-stage, chronic alcoholics." The American Indian Community Development Corporation's wet house is called Anishinabe Wakiagun. To live at Wakiagun, a resident must have been homeless for most of the past five years, been admitted to detox centers at least twenty times in the past three years, and have participated in at least two previous chemical dependency treatments. These facilities are not without controversy. One Hennepin County commissioner hated the idea that tax money was going into these places: "If we're going to provide you housing, you should figure out how to stop being drunk all the time." Still, an article in the *Journal of the American Medical Association* that year endorsed the wet house as cutting down trips to detox units, emergency rooms, and jail, and even helping curb drinking. Minneapolis is equally conflicted about how to deal with booze in the respectable parts of town. Voters in 2014 got rid of a rule in the city charter that neighborhood restaurants have to earn 70 percent of their income from food, but full-service bars are still forbidden in most of Minneapolis.

So the cycle continues. Minneapolis shuts down some establishments and clears out some blight and rejoices until the next problem spot breaks out and threatens the city's reputation as a family-friendly place. Our walking tour that July morning ended at the bland office block that replaced the Metropolitan Building, and I reminded the group that the city has never forgotten or forgiven the destruction of that monumental building. In 2011 journalists and historians marked the fiftieth anniversary of its demolition with reminiscences and regret, and the granite chunks of the building live on as decorations in a little park on Nicollet Avenue and next to a microbrewery in Northeast Minneapolis, like the relics of some dismembered saint.

No one preserved the bricks of the Victor Hotel, the window displays of Rex Liquors, or the pink plastic cushions of the Sourdough Bar. Johnny Rex would have denied it, but they are every bit as sacred to the city's memory.

ACKNOWLEDGMENTS

This book happened because John Bacich came to the phone to take my cold call in 2009. For the next three years, he opened his life and his personal archive to me, welcoming me into his sitting room even as his body failed. His wife, Barbara Lee Bacich, was an essential partner in this project, jogging and correcting Johnny's memory, retrieving photographs and files from the basement, and answering even the most painful questions. Along the way, Johnny and Barbara kept asking me what I would do with all this information, and even though I told them, I'm not sure they entirely believed me. I will always be grateful for their generosity, and I regret that Johnny and Barbara did not live to see this book in its final form.

The staff at the City of Minneapolis Department of Community Planning and Economic Development lugged several boxes out of storage and let me examine them in an unused office. Craig Steiner told me how I could get them. Camille Austad made me welcome at CPED headquarters. I was aided by Lydia Lucas's cataloging of CPED historical records. Those records now reside at the Hennepin County Library Special Collections, where they have a marvelous steward in Ted Hathaway. Ted and his colleague Ian Stade also helped me find records in the library's vast collections. The *Star Tribune*'s clipping and photo archives, maintained by my fellow Stribbers Sandy Date and John Wareham, were also crucial, as were the archives of the Minnesota Historical Society and Hennepin History Museum. Thor Anderson at Saving Tape performed his magic to convert Johnny's 16 mm film into HD video and forty-three thousand individual digital images.

I am grateful to Robert Jorvig, Samuel Wallace, and Michael

Rockland for sharing their memories in interviews. Rod Lazorik did that and more, sending me a VHS tape with his own edit of the *Skidrow* footage. Ronald Corwin provided a section of his privately published autobiography. I drew heavily on the fine work of other historians of the Gateway: David Rosheim, the late Judith Martin, Joseph Hart, and John Lightfoot, whose public television documentary *Down on Skid Row* brought Johnny's stories to a statewide audience. He also entrusted me with the box of snapshots of gandy dancers that helped start this whole thing off.

I can thank Erik Johnson for first introducing me to the world of Johnny Rex, by way of a VHS tape of the *Skidrow* documentary that he loaned me shortly after I moved to Minneapolis. Erik is also my fellow principal investigator on an unfunded, ongoing research project to document the last dive bars of Minneapolis. The smell of those places has definitely informed this book. Karl Herber, whose vocation is making beautiful photographs, gave me technical assistance and endured my endless prattle about the photographers of Skid Row.

I feel quite fortunate that this project landed at the University of Minnesota Press, where I could not ask for a better editor than Pieter Martin. Pieter tames my worst instincts as a writer. Kristian Tvedten helped me see the big (and small) pictures. Before he left the Press, Todd Orjala was an early supporter who helped me see how words and photographs can work together.

At times, especially in the later stages of this project, my family likely believed I had hit the skids. I owe an enormous debt to them, starting with my parents, Edward and Marion Shiffer, whose passion for books infected me at an early age. My children, Annika and Malachi Shiffer-Delegard, put up with their father's obsession, suffering through a walking tour of the old Gateway and entertaining themselves on research trips to the Minnesota History Center. Most of all, I am grateful to Kirsten Delegard, my soul mate, conversation partner, wonderful writer, brilliant editor, creator of the Historyapolis project, and a far more accomplished historian than I. She taught me everything I know about history, Minneapolis, archival research, book publishing, not to mention love and life and believing that I can actually complete something. For those and so many other reasons, I dedicate this book to her.

Notes

The King of Skid Row draws from the author's extensive interviews of John and Barbara Bacich from 2009 to 2012, as well as an unpublished memoir by John Bacich, dictated and transcribed in 2002 and 2003 and provided to the author. Material derived from the interviews and memoirs is not cited in the endnotes.

Introduction

Page 6: Lovald rented a room above a Gateway bar: Lovald, "From Hobohemia to Skid Row," 368.

Page 7: Liebling was well on his way to becoming a giant: Silberman, *The Gateway*, 8.

Page 7: Johnny Rex likely would never have known that his bar: Silberman, *The Gateway*, 12.

Page 10: Joseph Mitchell writes about a habitué: Mitchell, *Up in the Old Hotel*, 21.

Page 10: Johnny more closely resembled another New York character: Weegee, *Naked City*, 138–39.

1. Johnny Rex

Page 19: Liquor smuggled from Canada could travel: Maccabee, *John Dillinger Slept Here*, 25.

Page 19: The political culture was primed for corruption: Maccabee, *John Dillinger Slept Here*, 2.

Page 24: Aside from prostitutes swarming Hennepin Avenue: Lait and Mortimer, *U.S.A. Confidential*, 116.

Page 24: "We have seen all the dives in the land": Lait and Mortimer, *U.S.A. Confidential*, 116.

Page 25: The city thought major public works projects: Martin and Goddard, *Past Choices/Present Landscapes*, 53–54.

Page 28: In 1961 journalist and urban activist Jane Jacobs recognized: Jacobs, *The Death and Life of Great American Cities*, 338.

Page 28: Eager to keep their central business districts vibrant: Isenberg, *Downtown America*, 191.

Page 28: Cities eagerly tapped into that money: Avila, *The Folklore of the Freeway*, 91.

Page 28: A law passed in 1954 enabled federal funding: Isenberg, *Downtown America*, 192.

Page 29: In 1958 *Fortune* magazine could have been talking: Isenberg, *Downtown America*, 188.

Page 29: The crisis for Minnesota's largest city and economic capital: Hart and Hirschoff, *Down and Out*, 4.

Page 29: Robert Jorvig, the head of the city's Housing: Robert Jorvig, conversation with the author, November 3, 2013.

2. THE GANDIES

Page 33: "The skid rower does not bathe": Wallace, *Skid Row as a Way of Life*, 144.

Page 38: The Victor Hotel had a larger number of current: Lovald, "From Hobohemia to Skid Row," 279.

Page 39: A 1952 city report concluded that the denizens: *Survey of the Minneapolis Gateway*.

Page 39: "Who are these strangers within our Gateway?": Frank Murray, "Gateway Owes Bad Name to 'Fringe' Element," *Minneapolis Star*, September 28, 1953.

Page 39: Lovald observed five years later: Lovald, "From Hobohemia to Skid Row," 305, 407.

Page 40: They surveyed the neighborhood that month: Lovald, "From Hobohemia to Skid Row," 248.

Page 40: Lovald offered a guide to their fashion no-nos: Lovald, "From Hobohemia to Skid Row," 306.

Page 40: "Perhaps the single most distinguishing mark": Lovald, "From Hobohemia to Skid Row," 307.

Page 40: Jack Kerr, a resident of the Oslo Hotel: "Warm Night Helps Thief," *Minneapolis Star*, July 1, 1958.

Page 41: Jim Wiggins, who worked at the Senate Bar: Joseph Hart, "Room at the Bottom," *City Pages,* May 6, 1998.

Page 45: "A frequent conversation filled with reminiscences": Lovald, "From Hobohemia to Skid Row," 439.

Page 47: "Homosexuality—especially among tramps": Lovald, "From Hobohemia to Skid Row," 422–23.

Page 48: The Dugout Bar, a few blocks: Van Cleve, *Land of 10,000 Loves,* 65.

Page 48: The *Minneapolis Star* blamed it on penicillin: Jay Edgerton, "Wonder Drug Abets Skid Row Vice," *Minneapolis Star,* July 12, 1955.

Page 49: The Minneapolis Police Morals Squad targeted: "Raids Gather 30 Women at Three Bars," *Minneapolis Tribune,* January 24, 1958.

Page 49: The city's new health director was determined to end: Edgerton, "Wonder Drug Abets Skid Row Vice."

Page 49: Dr. Karl Lundeberg was a preacher's son: "Health Chief Is Retiring," *Minneapolis Star,* September 19, 1964.

Page 49: Lundeberg used the language of crime: memorandum from Karl Lundeberg to Mayor Arthur Naftalin, November 1, 1962.

Page 51: Lundeberg soon narrowed down: "Two Bars Face License Loss in Disease Cases," *Minneapolis Star,* October 29, 1958.

Page 51: That October, the health director stood up: "Two Bars Face License Loss in Disease Cases."

Page 53: At the Beacon Hotel, Merrick met Elmer Kistler: Martin Merrick, "Men of Skid Row: 'We'll Move, but We Want to Stay Together,'" *Minneapolis Star,* October 10, 1958.

Page 53: A block away from the Beacon Hotel, Pioneer Hotel proprietor: Merrick, "Men of Skid Row."

Page 55: At a public hearing in December 1958: Abe Altrowitz, "Move for Lower Loopers Opposed," *Minneapolis Star,* Dec. 23, 1958; "Site for Relocating Skid Row Residents Attacked, Defended," *Minneapolis Tribune,* December 23, 1958.

Page 56: Over the next year, Mr. Skid Row kept showing up: Abe Altrowitz, "Park Commissioners Oppose Charter Change," *Minneapolis Star,* May 21, 1959; Abe Altrowitz, "Appointive Posts Called Boost for Voter Apathy," *Minneapolis Star,* October 29, 1959.

Page 56: In early 1959, he wrote in a widely circulated handbill: Rosheim, *The Other Minneapolis,* 187.

Page 57: By September 1959, he is listed: Ted Kolderie, "Study Shows Job of Lower Loop Moving Lies Ahead," *Minneapolis Tribune*, September 18, 1959.

3. RING IN THE BOOZE

Page 61: "The bartender acts as a kind of guardian": Wallace, *Skid Row as a Way of Life*, 71.

Page 61: In 1884 the city drew a line around the downtown: Jim Hathaway, "The Liquor Patrol Limits of Minneapolis."

Page 63: Each ward's elected representative: Hathaway, "The Liquor Patrol Limits of Minneapolis."

Page 63: A 1952 survey found an astonishing sixty-two bars: *Survey of the Minneapolis Gateway*.

Page 63: One researcher made the following observation: Lovald, "From Hobohemia to Skid Row," 414.

Page 63: The wettest block of all was Block 10: Lovald, "From Hobohemia to Skid Row," 237.

Page 66: The Kefauver Crime Commission labeled Kid Cann: Maccabee, "Alias Kid Cann."

Page 66: The real money lay in thirty-seven liquor: Jim Hathaway, "The Liquor Patrol Limits of Minneapolis."

Page 67: Its proprietor, Joe Wolk, was a bookie: *Minneapolis Tribune*, January 20, 1953.

Page 67: The city had held that distinction: Davies and Abram, *Betting the Line*, 55–56.

Page 67: One night in 1953, an armed lunatic: "Police Trace Record of Gunman Wounded in Gun Battle at City Hall," *Minneapolis Star*, September 28, 1953.

Page 70: A young man named Frederick Ironeyes: "Liquor Stolen, Suspect Charged," *Minneapolis Tribune*, February 19, 1959.

Page 70: Bottle gangs were an established: Lovald, "From Hobohemia to Skid Row," 418.

Page 71: Once a group obtained enough funds: Wallace, *Skid Row as a Way of Life*, 203.

Page 72: Skid Row specialized in "white tile bars": J. T. Hathaway, "The Evolution of Drinking Places in the Twin Cities," 336.

Page 72: The sociology students, in their exhaustive research: Lovald, "From Hobohemia to Skid Row," 417.

Page 72: it was "one of the raunchiest operations in town": Frank Premack, "Smull Plans New Night Spot," *Minneapolis Tribune,* March 7, 1963.

Page 74: He controlled, at one time or another: Al McConagha, "Smull Group Saloons Near End in Gateway," *Minneapolis Tribune,* December 16, 1962.

Page 74: Smull eventually did get caught up: "Here Is a List of Cases Dismissed," *Minneapolis Tribune,* September 12, 1961.

Page 78: In 1956 a truck driver visiting: "Truck Driver Misses $495 as Date Departs," *Minneapolis Tribune,* November 5, 1956.

Page 78: A similar fate greeted a Montana trucker: "Woman Called Lure in Slugging, $1266 robbery," *Minneapolis Tribune,* July 6, 1957.

Page 79: In 1956 Vivian Littlesoldier, a twenty-seven-year-old: "Woman Treated after Beating," *Minneapolis Star,* November 21, 1956.

Page 79: In 1959 a patron of the Bridge Square Bar: "St. Paul Man Wins Tag Match, but Loses $20," *Minneapolis Tribune,* June 29, 1959.

Page 79: One place, the Great Lakes Bar, had a different: Rosheim, *The Other Minneapolis,* 190.

Page 79: In 1957 a full 44 percent of people arrested: Lovald, "From Hobohemia to Skid Row," 310.

Page 79: Macalester College anthropologist James Spradley: Spradley, *You Owe Yourself a Drunk,* 252.

Page 81: One of Spradley's main confidants was William Tanner: Spradley, *You Owe Yourself a Drunk,* 26.

Page 83: One bad summer night, a man went into a phone booth: "Woman Stabbed in Barroom Fight," *Minneapolis Tribune,* September 20, 1959.

4. THE FLOPHOUSE

Page 87: "It does not matter how small a cubicle is": Orwell, *Down and Out in Paris and London,* 154.

Page 89: Minneapolis's first cage hotel appeared: Lovald, "From Hobohemia to Skid Row," 107.

Page 89: The former head of the Union City Mission: Lovald, "From Hobohemia to Skid Row," 106.

Page 90: In cities across the nation, similar low-rent lodging districts: Groth, *Living Downtown,* 131.

Page 91: It wasn't unusual in those days: Groth, *Living Downtown,* 16.

Page 93: Yet an estimated eighteen thousand men (and six hundred women): Lovald, "From Hobohemia to Skid Row," 265.

Page 93: A 1963 survey in Chicago found more than seventy-five hundred: Groth, *Living Downtown*, 146.

Page 93: But this kind of community, with many uses: Groth, *Living Downtown*, 201–8.

Page 93: As early as the 1890s, Minneapolis began to worry: "History Lesson concerning Lower Loop Improvement," Minneapolis Housing and Redevelopment Authority, undated memo.

Page 93: In 1918 the city outlawed the opening: Martin and Goddard, *Past Choices/Present Landscapes*, 53.

Page 93: "The Nicollet Hotel, the city's finest": Lait and Mortimer, *U.S.A. Confidential*, 116.

Page 94: A graduate student wandering through the Gateway: Lovald, "From Hobohemia to Skid Row," 395.

Page 94: One resident described the accommodations: Rosheim, *The Other Minneapolis*, 170.

Page 94: One gandy had a pair of shoes that apparently: Rosheim, *The Other Minneapolis*, 170.

Page 95: Back in 1958, Samuel Wallace paid sixty cents: Wallace, *Skid Row as a Way of Life*, 39.

Page 97: Graduate student Keith Lovald cataloged the more exotic: Lovald, "From Hobohemia to Skid Row," 396.

Page 97: A man by the name of Amen Balkin lived in a flop: "Money by the Sackful," *Minneapolis Star*, May 24, 1955.

Page 97: In November 1957, a visitor to Minneapolis: "Six Men Held in Beating, Robbery," *Minneapolis Star*, November 18, 1957.

Page 99: "As a matter of fact," Lovald wrote: Lovald, "From Hobohemia to Skid Row," 398.

Page 99: A scene captured by one of the eavesdropping: Wallace, *Skid Row as a Way of Life*, 37–38.

Page 100: Some of the flophouses featured signs: Wallace, *Skid Row as a Way of Life*, 38.

Page 100: In another unconventional research exercise: Wallace, *Skid Row as a Way of Life*, 38.

Page 100: On a February night in 1957, a man was discovered: "Clerk Held in Beating of Two," *Minneapolis Star*, February 8, 1957.

Page 101: Two months after that fracas: "11 Fined for Liquor Bout," *Minneapolis Star*, April 6, 1957.

Page 101: Two night clerks at the A&C Hotel: "Man, 26, Jailed after Attack," *Minneapolis Star,* March 7, 1953.

Page 103: Big Mose at one time was the most feared: Friendly, *Minnesota Rag,* 40–57.

Page 103: On a cold day in 1953, a fire at the A&C: "Proprietor Bats for His Nine," *Minneapolis Star,* February 28, 1953.

Page 105: It turns out judges were some of the people: Jerry Kirshenbaum, "Big Mose Lies Dead in City Where He Saw a Lot of Life," *Minneapolis Tribune,* March 28, 1965.

Page 106: The flophouses "are filled with the old": Wallace, *Skid Row as a Way of Life,* 36.

Page 106: In March 1956, Alvin Opsal lived: "His Bed on Fire," *Minneapolis Star,* March 12, 1956; "Man Overcome by Smoke, Dies," *Minneapolis Star,* March 14, 1956.

Page 106: In 1959 Leonard D. Gladstone got sixty days: "Seven-Time Loser Gets 60 Day Term," *Minneapolis Star,* January 21, 1959.

Page 106: In 1955 one of my predecessors: Jay Edgerton, "Health Officers Fight Skid Row Filth," *Minneapolis Star,* July 14, 1955.

Page 109: "The odor of these overused toilets mingled": Hart and Hirschoff, *Down and Out,* 27.

Page 109: Lovald's nose detected the cuisine from illegal hot plates: Lovald, "From Hobohemia to Skid Row," 396.

Page 109: At times, though, he found the smell: Lovald, "From Hobohemia to Skid Row," 321.

Page 110: By 2000 only about eight flophouses: Isay and Abramson, *Flophouse,* xiii–xiv.

Page 111: One of those establishments, the old Prince Hotel: Dan Barry, "At Bowery House Hotel, Cultures Clash as the Shabby Meet the Shabby Chic," *New York Times,* October 12, 2011.

5. Missions

Page 115: "If you don't start behaving like a Christian": Wallace, *Skid Row as a Way of Life,* 59.

Page 116: "The men on Skid Row seem to sense": Wallace, *Skid Row as a Way of Life,* 56.

Page 116: In the early part of the twentieth century, the missions' precursors: Groth, *Living Downtown,* 148.

Page 116: In 1911 Minneapolis opened its lodging house: Lovald, "From Hobohemia to Skid Row," 114.

Page 116: Once it closed, the missions moved in: Lovald, "From Hobohemia to Skid Row," 117.

Page 118: No fewer than nine rescue missions: Lovald, "From Hobohemia to Skid Row," 427.

Page 118: "My heart, listen, you won't believe it": Wallace, *Skid Row as a Way of Life*, 53.

Page 118: "When you go out this door tonight": Wallace, *Skid Row as a Way of Life*, 57.

Page 118: If the preacher went on too long, the congregation: Wallace, *Skid Row as a Way of Life*, 59–60.

Page 118: Committing to the mission meant: Wallace, *Skid Row as a Way of Life*, 61.

Page 120: A mission worker in the late 1950s gave his view: Wallace, *Skid Row as a Way of Life*, 57.

Page 120: To our great fortune, Samuel Wallace preserved: Wallace, *Skid Row as a Way of Life*, 112.

Page 120: Restaurants also served something called "coffee-ans": Lovald, "From Hobohemia to Skid Row," 379.

Page 120: One former Gateway resident even showed up: *Report on the Relocation of Residents, Businesses, and Institutions from the Gateway Project Area.*

Page 122: One of them, a Norwegian immigrant named Marie Sandvik: Rosheim, *The Other Minneapolis*, 163.

Page 122: Paul was a towering figure: "Dr. W. E. Paul, Forgotten Men's Friend, Dies on Lonely Roadside," *Minneapolis Tribune,* January 5, 1955.

Page 122: Founded in 1895 by a coalition of Protestant churches: "Outline of Union City Mission Activities." Fact sheet, publication date unknown. Union City Mission file, Minneapolis Collection, Hennepin County Central Library.

Page 123: Paul was dubbed a "rebuilder of men": Cleo Fenton Nichols, "Rebuilding Men." Article from unknown publication and date, Union City Mission file.

Page 123: The cover of the ticket book carried a number of pointers: Union City Mission file.

Page 124: Working undercover, sociology graduate student William Eckland: Wallace, *Skid Row as a Way of Life*, 66.

Page 125: Professor Theodore Caplow, chairman: Lovald, "From Hobohemia to Skid Row," 222.

Page 125: In the spring of 1958, Professor Caplow began: Wallace, *Skid Row as a Way of Life*, viii–ix.

Page 126: "The police promptly picked me up": Samuel Wallace, conversation with the author, October 12, 2011.

Page 126: "One was a disgusting, dirty haven": Corwin, *The Good Life*.

Page 127: He put on his "scuzziest" clothes: Michael Rockland, conversation with the author, October 8, 2013.

Page 127: In September 1959, Lovald got a room in the Washington Hotel: Lovald, "From Hobohemia to Skid Row," 368.

Page 128: Out on the street, they recorded the panhandler's scripts: Lovald, "From Hobohemia to Skid Row," 372.

Page 128: In what must have been a vile: Lovald, "From Hobohemia to Skid Row," 283.

Page 130: "It should not be forgotten that a bulldozer": Lovald, "From Hobohemia to Skid Row," 449.

Page 130: A little over two years later, a familiar tune: Dick Caldwell, "Skid Row Has Its Last Public Christmas Party," *Minneapolis Star*, December 11, 1962.

Page 130: Five months after the Christmas party: Maurice Hobbs, "Where Once Men Lived . . . Empty Rooms. Mission, Hotel Give Way to Progress," *Minneapolis Star*, May 11, 1963.

6. THE LOST CITY

Page 134: A fire had broken out in the back of the saloon: "Firemen Plagued by Smoke, Spectators," *Minneapolis Star*, July 21, 1961; "Fire Sweeps Lower Loop Hotel, Bar," *Minneapolis Tribune*, July 21, 1961.

Page 136: A grand jury was investigating Minneapolis's notoriously: "Johnson Pleads Innocent to Charge of Accepting Bribe," *Minneapolis Star*, June 22, 1961.

Page 139: "They state that rats have, through the 75": Abe Altrowitz, "Gateway Picture Shows Hazards, Rats, Derelicts," *Minneapolis Star*, February 14, 1952.

Page 139: The vast majority were single men: Gazzolo, "Skid Row Gives Renewalists Rough, Tough Relocation Problems."

Page 141: The HRA felt the policy was perhaps too harsh: Jorvig, conversation with the author, November 3, 2013.

Page 141: If the men found a new place to live and came back: Gazzolo, "Skid Row Gives Renewalists Rough, Tough Relocation Problems."

Page 141: The agency's larger ambition: Gazzolo, "Skid Row Gives Renewalists Rough, Tough Relocation Problems."

Page 141: It started with the Vendome Hotel: "The Old and the New," *Minneapolis Star,* October 23, 1959; Hart and Hirschoff, *Down and Out,* 2.

Page 142: A few years later, a city brochure exulted: *Gateway Center Progress Report Number 3.*

Page 142: Relocating his liquor business: "Council Group Turns Down Two Liquor License Applications," *Minneapolis Star,* November 20, 1961.

Page 142: Someone brought up the old claim: "Council Group Turns Down Two Liquor License Applications," *Minneapolis Star,* November 20, 1961.

Page 144: Wolinski had just arrived: Frank Premack and Jim Parsons, "Landlord Slain, Ex-Alderman Wounded by Liquor Store Owner," *Minneapolis Tribune,* September 16, 1962.

Page 146: In 1976 Johnny picked up a copy of the *Minneapolis Tribune*: Joe Rigert, Nick Coleman, and Robert Sullwold, "Ex-Liquor Store Owner Finds More Profit in Owning Buildings," *Minneapolis Tribune,* April 14, 1976.

Page 146: Later that year, he picked up the paper again: Patricia Marx, "Records of Liquor Operation Seized," *Minneapolis Star,* June 4, 1976.

Page 148: People mourned the loss of a landmark: Millett, *Lost Twin Cities,* 222–25; Jorvig, conversation with the author.

Page 148: He was haunted by the "recurring dream landscape": Rosheim, *The Other Minneapolis,* 1.

Page 148: That description sounds much more soulful than its replacement: Rosheim, *The Other Minneapolis,* 196.

Page 149: Rosheim found out about Johnny: Rosheim, *The Other Minneapolis,* 172.

Page 149: Writing in 1989, two professors at the University of Minnesota: Martin and Goddard, *Past Choices/Present Landscapes,* 67

Page 150: In August 2011, a film lover named Peter Schilling: Schilling, "Down and Out (in New York and Minneapolis)," *The Bug* (blog), http://

mudvillemagazine.com/wordpress/2011/08/01/down-and-out-in-new
-york-and-minneapolis, accessed January 31, 2015.

Epilogue

Page 156: Nearly three decades after the city leaders gathered: Dennis J. McGrath, "Block E 'Demolition' Signals High Hopes," *Minneapolis Star Tribune,* October 18, 1988.

Page 156: The city ultimately paid $39 million to build the new Block E: Janet Moore and Eric Roper, "If Not a Casino, What's Plan B for Block E?," *Minneapolis Star Tribune,* January 30, 2012.

Page 157: Yet its modern counterpart is the "wet house": Bob Shaw, "At St. Paul 'Wet House,' Liquor Can Be Their Life—and Death," *St. Paul Pioneer Press,* December 5, 2010; Kevin Duchschere, "'Wethouses': Not Always Sober, but Safe," *Minneapolis Star Tribune,* August 12, 2009.

Page 157: Still, an article in the *Journal of the American Medical Association*: Larimer et al., "Health Care and Public Service Use and Costs."

Page 157: Voters in 2014 got rid of a rule in the city charter: Erin Golden, "Minneapolis Voters Scrap Alcohol Ratios, Raise Filing Fees," *Minneapolis Star Tribune,* November 4, 2014.

Page 157: In 2011 journalists and historians marked the fiftieth anniversary: Rick Nelson, "They Paved Paradise," *Minneapolis Star Tribune,* December 11, 2011.

Bibliography

Avila, Eric. *The Folklore of the Freeway: Race and Revolt in the Modernist City.* Minneapolis: University of Minnesota Press, 2014.

Corwin, Ronald. *The Good Life.* Privately published, 2011.

Davies, Richard O., and Richard G. Abram. *Betting the Line: Sports Wagering in American Life.* Columbus: Ohio State University Press, 2001.

Friendly, Fred. *Minnesota Rag: The Dramatic Story of the Landmark Supreme Court Case That Gave New Meaning to Freedom of the Press.* New York: Random House, 1981.

Gateway Center Progress Report Number 3. Minneapolis: Minneapolis Housing and Redevelopment Authority, January 1965.

Gazzolo, Dorothy. "Skid Row Gives Renewalists Rough, Tough, Relocation Problems." *Journal of Housing* 18 (August–September 1961): 327.

Groth, Paul. *Living Downtown: The History of Residential Hotels in the United States.* Berkeley: University of California Press, 1999.

Hart, Joseph, and Edwin Hirschoff. *Down and Out: The Life and Death of Minneapolis's Skid Row.* Minneapolis: University of Minnesota Press, 2002.

Hathaway, J. T. "The Evolution of Drinking Places in the Twin Cities, from the Advent of White Settlement to the Present." PhD diss., University of Minnesota, 1982.

Hathaway, Jim. "The Liquor Patrol Limits of Minneapolis." *Hennepin County History* 44, no. 3 (Fall 1985): 9–10.

Isay, David, and Stacy Abramson. *Flophouse: Life on the Bowery.* New York: Random House, 2000.

Isenberg, Alison. *Downtown America: A History of the Place and the People Who Made It.* Chicago: University of Chicago Press, 2004.

Jacobs, Jane. *The Death and Life of Great American Cities.* New York: Vintage Books, 1961.

Lait, Jack, and Lee Mortimer. *U.S.A. Confidential.* New York: Crown Publishers, 1952.

Larimer, Mary E., et al. "Health Care and Public Service Use and Costs before and after Provision of Housing for Chronically Homeless Persons with Severe Alcohol Problems." *JAMA* 301, no. 13 (2009): 1349–57.

Lovald, Keith. "From Hobohemia to Skid Row: The Changing Community of the Homeless Man." PhD diss., University of Minnesota, 1960.

Maccabee, Paul. "Alias Kid Cann." *Minneapolis–St. Paul Magazine,* November 1991.

———. *John Dillinger Slept Here: A Crook's Tour of Crime and Corruption in St. Paul, 1920–1936.* St. Paul: Minnesota Historical Society Press, 1995.

Martin, Judith, and Anthony Goddard. *Past Choices / Present Landscapes: The Impact of Urban Renewal on the Twin Cities.* Minneapolis: University of Minnesota Center for Urban and Regional Affairs, 1989.

Millett, Larry. *Lost Twin Cities.* St. Paul: Minnesota Historical Society Press, 1992.

Mitchell, Joseph. *Up in the Old Hotel.* New York: Pantheon Books, 1992.

Orwell, George. *Down and Out in Paris and London.* New York: Berkeley Medallion Books, 1967.

Report on the Relocation of Residents, Businesses, and Institutions from the Gateway Project Area. Minneapolis: Minneapolis Housing and Redevelopment Authority, November 1963.

Rosheim, David L. *The Other Minneapolis: A History of the Minneapolis Skid Row.* Maquoketa, Iowa: Andromeda Press, 1978.

Silberman, Robert. *The Gateway.* Minneapolis: Center for Book Arts, 1993.

Spradley, James. *You Owe Yourself a Drunk: An Ethnography of Urban Nomads.* Long Grove, Ill.: Waveland Press, 1970.

A Survey of the Minneapolis Gateway. Minneapolis: Community Planning and Economic Development Department, 1952.

Van Cleve, Stewart. *Land of 10,000 Loves: A History of Queer Minnesota.* Minneapolis: University of Minnesota Press, 2012.

Wallace, Samuel. *Skid Row as a Way of Life.* Totowa, N.J.: Bedminster Press, 1965.

Weegee. *Naked City.* New York: Essential Books, 1945.

Index

JAMES ELI SHIFFER is a columnist and editor at the Minneapolis–St. Paul *Star Tribune*. In 2010, he partnered with Ewen Media to create *Rubbed Out,* a multimedia history of the murder of a Minneapolis journalist in 1945. He lives in Minneapolis with his wife and children.